Bhikkhu Basnagoda Rahula, Ph.D.

Beautiful Living

Buddha's Way to Prosperity, Wisdom, and Inner Peace

Foreword:

Sir Arthur C. Clarke

VIMAMSA
PUBLISHERS

Houston
2006

Vimamsa Publishers
P.O. Box 753231
Houston, Texas 77275

ISBN: 0-9772343-0-4
Library of Congress Control Number: 2005932234

Printed in the United States of America
Design and layout: e-Cobo.com

Wise laypeople improve two kinds of skills. First, they develop the ability to obtain new wealth and to secure the acquired wealth. Next, they learn how to differentiate between wholesome and unwholesome conduct and how to follow a wholesome way of life.

Lay followers of my teaching secure a tenfold improvement. [In their external progress], they [develop skill to] obtain more property, increase wealth, improve family relationships, establish a strong workforce, and obtain more four-footed animals [such as horses and sheep]. [In their inner growth], my lay followers develop confidence in their spiritual path, discipline themselves, acquire more knowledge, practice generosity, and gain wisdom.

Buddha, the *Gradual Sayings*

Contents

Foreword

I have to admit that there is some incongruity in a lifelong secularist like myself writing these words to introduce a book on Buddha's way to prosperity, wisdom, and inner peace. My views on religion have been widely publicized, and I believe all religions are a form of mind virus that affects otherwise healthy—and often educated—human beings.

Buddhism stands apart in being tolerant, accommodating, and pragmatic. Having lived for a half-century in Sri Lanka, I have seen how Buddha's teachings are applied by various groups in many different ways. Strange as it might seem, perfectly rational people and rabid fundamentalists both claim to derive their beliefs and attitudes from the same source. Clearly, many liberties are being taken with the original teachings.

That is why I welcome the publication of this book, by Dr. Bhikkhu Basnagoda Rahula, which aims to rediscover the principles and values of Buddhism that have been obscured by centuries of culture and history.

Many years ago, I had the pleasure of associating with the late Dr. Walpola Rahula, one of the few truly erudite people I have met. He struggled long and hard to rid Buddhism of fanaticism and rituals. I hope the current Bhikkhu Rahula will continue that noble mission, as there is much unfinished business.

Sir Arthur C. Clarke
Fellow, King's College, London
October 15, 2005

Preface

Determined to bring benefits and happiness to a great number of people, Buddha established a well-organized society. This social movement attracted hundreds of thousands of men and women who belonged to all social classes. Buddha's new society consisted of two groups: ordained disciples and lay followers. Buddha considered both groups equally important in his society. He made every effort to lead his ordained disciples to the highest spiritual progress and to guide his lay followers toward prosperity, wisdom, and inner peace.

Yet history buried a part of his guidance! The passage of twenty-six centuries made Buddha's teaching for the lay community insignificant, obscure, and misleading. We intend to restore it. Breaking through historical and cultural barriers, we strive to trace what Buddha actually taught for the benefit of his lay followers. This book, which identifies, regroups, and elaborates on Buddha's speeches about lay life, marks the culmination of our effort.

Numerous requests from various quarters germinated and fertilized the seed for this work. Audiences at my public speeches, in particular, frequently requested that I write a book about Buddha's philosophy for, and complete guidance of, lay life. Considering the scarcity of similar work and the usefulness of such a book to society, I ventured to undertake that task. This book is the result.

Chapter organization

A brief description about the chapter organization seems necessary in order to present an overview of this book. Chapter One examines the causes behind the obscurity and misinterpretation of Buddha's guidance of the layperson's life. This chapter is important because it

answers the question of why Buddha's teaching for everyday life has
so far drawn little attention. Truths often remain hidden, sometimes
for millenniums, due to the course of history. When we discover such
truths, we may also need to explain why they remained hidden for so
long. To fulfill this need, Chapter One briefly expounds the reasons
behind the obscurity and the misinterpretation of Buddha's teaching
for lay life.

Chapter Two specifically focuses on the freedom Buddha offered to
the layperson to be prosperous. This chapter basically denies the popular but clearly erroneous view that Buddha discouraged one's endeavor
for success. Based on this false view, some mistakenly believe that to
be wealthy means to go against Buddha's teaching. This misunderstanding may present Buddha's teaching as being mostly irrelevant to
the layperson's life. The purpose of Chapter Two is to help the reader
understand the conditional freedom Buddha offered to the layperson
to achieve prosperity.

The rest of the book discusses the requirements that Buddha identified as vital for a successful and peaceful life. He clarified virtually
everything that would make a layperson's life prosperous, meaningful,
and peaceful. Chapter Three begins the discussion of these instructions, techniques, and tips, focusing on how to initiate one's journey
toward material success. Chapters Four through Thirteen continue to
elaborate on various topics that Buddha identified as important for a
layperson's success. Basically, these chapters discuss what Buddha offered for a layperson's personal and social relationships, decision making, and personality development.

The final chapter brings the discussion to the most important
topic: how to achieve inner peace and happiness. As Buddha emphasized, achievement of happiness should be the ultimate goal in life. He
introduced effective techniques to reach this goal, which is elusive but
feasible. His techniques may be revealing to many people who might
be confused about the means of obtaining inner peace and happiness.

The foremost thought behind this book is to present practical and helpful instructions for the reader's daily life. Therefore, the contents have been selected, organized, and designed to serve this purpose. Metaphysical concepts, in particular, have been omitted because they represent an altogether different field. Anyone looking for practical guidance to prosperity, wisdom, and inner peace will find this book extremely beneficial.

Translations

Almost every translation of the Pali texts used in this work is original. New, reliable translations are now being published, but some existent translations fail to present the correct meanings of important Pali words and phrases. Some also lack clarity and simplicity. Again, word-for-word translations of Pali passages neither convey their original meaning nor preserve their original tone. These difficulties prompted me to spend hours with Pali scholars in an effort to present the best possible meaning of the Pali quotations used in this book.

Several salient characteristics of the translations given in this book are worth mentioning. One is the avoidance of repetition. In the original Pali texts, some sentences and phrases are redundant, making a word-for-word translation of these passages meaningless. Therefore, I have omitted repetitions in an effort to convey the clearest meaning without being wordy.

Further, most quotations used in the book give the best possible meanings of the Pali passages, not direct translations. For instance, on page 8, the English rendition reads "Master, we are the laypeople who live with a family . . ." The Pali phrase for "live with a family" is *puttadara sambadhasayanam ajjhavasama.* This phrase literally means "sleep together in a bed where children and wife cause disturbances." What the speaker actually wants to say is that he has a family to whom he must fulfill his duties. Thus, "live with a family" seems to be the most relevant equivalent of the Pali phrase. I have followed this method of translating throughout the book.

Also, the translations have been adapted in keeping with modern linguistic norms, particularly with gender impartiality, clarity, and simplicity. Such pronoun references as "he or she" and "his or her" are meant to avoid gender bias. Singular nouns in some original quotations have been changed into the plural in order to avoid the repetition of singular pronoun references. Long and complex Pali sentences have been divided into two or more short, simple sentences without changing their meaning.

The sources of translations are given in the endnotes. Some quotations may occur in several Pali Suttas, but only one source has been cited. Special notes appear with endnotes whenever the translation requires an explanation.

Citation of Sources

The generally accepted method of citation is to use the Pali Suttas published by the Pali Text Society. To refer to a quotation from the *Digha Nikaya 1*, for instance, a writer may note: DN I, (page number), PTS. Because Pali texts printed by the Pali Text Society are unavailable to most readers, citation of the PTS page numbers may not be helpful.

To avoid this inconvenience, this book gives the place, number, and name of Pali sources (e.g.: *Digha Nikaya III*: 31: Sigalovada Sutta). When the name does not appear in the original Pali texts, the original numerical order has been cited. This method of citation may help an interested reader to find the original sources, especially from an Internet search.

This book does not use symbols with Pali words to aid pronunciation. Since the objective of using Pali quotations and original Pali texts is to authenticate and clarify the points discussed, a pronunciation guide to Pali words does not seem necessary.

Thanks

Several renowned personalities have written about this book. Most prominent among them is communications satellite pioneer and science fiction guru Sir Arthur C. Clarke. I am honored to have the foreword from this legendary writer, whose books have mesmerized and enlightened the entire world.

Ven. Henepola Gunaratana Thero, a writer on Buddha's teaching and a well-known meditation teacher in America, and Anne C. Klein, professor of Buddhist studies at Rice University in Houston, Texas, wrote reviews. I thank them sincerely for showing their appreciation of this work.

Many persons have helped me in this undertaking. Among them, Ven. Pannila Ananda Nayaka Thero, Ven. Udagama Sumangala Thero, Saroja Gunaratne, Nalaka Gunawardena, Anuruddha Kulatunga, Nihal Rajakaruna, Nalaka Senaratne, Errol Wirasinghe, Kanishka deSilva, Shirin Wright, Nikolay Dimitrov, Ann Marie Gordon, and Gamini Wickramage are special for their useful comments and assistance. Shirin, in particular, has offered her excellent editing skills, Nikolay has designed this book beautifully, and Ann has provided a great book production service with United Graphics, Inc. Gamini has volunteered to design an attractive Web page (www.vimamsa.com) to promote this book. I thank them wholeheartedly.

Bhikkhu Basnagoda Rahula
Houston, Texas
October 30, 2005

Chapter One
....
A Treasure Buried in History

The moon, the sun, and my teaching . . .

They all shine brightly when they are

uncovered.

Buddha, the *Kindred Sayings*

For some readers, "Buddha's Guidance to Beautiful Living" might be an altogether new and unusual topic. They may have embraced the common assumption that Buddha taught about impermanence, suffering, and denial of pleasure. Influenced by this belief, they may assume that Buddha ignored happiness in lay life and discouraged people from seeking success. The most popular belief is that Buddha advised his listeners to renounce worldly pleasure and to seek happiness in spiritual life, not in their daily experience.

However, an in-depth study of Buddha's speeches reveals that this interpretation fails to present an accurate view of his teaching. Buddha clearly recognized and admired happiness in life. He both encouraged people to obtain wealth and instructed them on how to save, invest, and manage their wealth. He also offered guidance to his lay community for successful interpersonal and social relationships, decision making, and healthy personality development. Above all, he showed the lay community the path to happiness. Contrary to what some might believe today, Buddha's teaching includes invaluable instructions for success and happiness in everyday life.

Why worldly life became so important in Buddha's teaching

A curious reader might ask at this point why Buddha, the founder of a religion, focused so much on secular life. Such a question seems relevant since most readers might expect a religion to have a system of beliefs beyond sensory experience rather than a system of guidance for worldly life. However, this question arises only when we interpret Buddha's teaching in terms of what the word "religion" means. Notably, Buddha's teaching was a different approach to religion. Both the basic philosophy of his teaching and unique social factors in the sixth century B.C. paved the way for Buddha not only to guide his listeners' spiritual progress but also to oversee their daily lives.

How did Buddha's philosophy influence his approach to worldly life? Buddha never presented himself or his disciples as messengers or representatives of a divine power. Therefore, the importance of his teaching to society had to be demonstrated mainly in terms of its social usefulness. A Brahmin teacher in Buddha's society would recommend and direct a huge offering to a deity to avert an impending catastrophe, but Buddha refused to stress such beliefs and practices. He would recommend human effort and human responsibility as the key to deal with difficult situations. Whenever a listener raised a question about his or her personal life, Buddha analyzed it and offered a solution based on human responsibility and human skill. Because Buddha and his ordained disciples constantly offered such rational solutions to the problems of their lay followers, "Worldly Life" became a popular topic in Buddha's teaching.

Moreover, social expectations further encouraged Buddha to focus on topics pertaining to daily life. Buddha lived in an age during which hundreds of thinkers and religious leaders were competing for followers. Some of those campaigners argued openly against spiritualism. They persuaded people to believe that such concepts as enlightenment, after-death existence, and rebirth were myths. As a result, Buddha's society had become so atheistic and secular that most people found their present life more attractive than after-death existence.

His audiences told Buddha about their expectations and inquired whether Buddha would have anything to offer for their worldly success. They were more attentive to those who provided assistance in their everyday lives than to those who talked about what follows death. Since Buddha's teaching ideally suited such a society, he relentlessly applied his philosophy toward the benefit of his lay community. This practice added more depth to the topic of worldly life in Buddha's teaching.

The prosperity of Buddha's society, in the meantime, resulted in secular life becoming a broad and profound subject in his teaching. The sixth century B.C. was an age of renaissance in India. Business people carried on extensive trading with Persia and the Greek world by both land and sea. With business booming and wealth increasing, affluent communities in Magadha and Kosala, the two states in which Buddha traveled widely, expanded. Consequently, topics such as business management, family life, social relationships, and decision making emerged as important aspects in daily life. Buddha, with his power, popularity, and rational approach to these topics, distinguished himself in that society as the most qualified adviser to the lay community. Thus, the subject of worldly life attained great prominence in his teaching.

Buddha had to play an especially active role in nurturing the prosperous lay community. Buddha's ordained community could not have existed without affluent lay supporters. Neither Buddha nor his ordained disciples were ascetics who practiced self-torture. Instead, they were social campaigners who lived a moderate life, avoiding both self-denial and self-indulgence. For the welfare of his ordained disciples, Buddha freely accepted lands and houses donated by the wealthy. Invited by his rich admirers, he regularly visited palaces and mansions for meals, often with hundreds of Bhikkhus. With the existence of his ordained community resting upon the prosperity of his lay supporters, Buddha found it essential to guide the material success of his lay followers.

Some of Buddha's most faithful followers and supporters were kings, princes, and business people who strove to increase their wealth and satisfy their senses. Happiness in everyday life was their main topic. King Kosala, for instance, often asked Buddha such questions as "Which sense should be satisfied most?"[1] Many others inquired about how they could make their lives happier. Buddha's own relationships with the wealthy seem to have inspired his approach to various aspects of secular life.

Given this unique social background, "Success and Happiness in Secular Life" became an important topic in Buddha's teaching. He volunteered to help families in various ways in their daily life. He also persuaded his ordained disciples to be engaged in the same task.

Buddha's attitude toward happiness in secular life

Buddha viewed the subject of happiness realistically, as something that actually existed. Addressing his ordained disciples to encourage their search for happiness in the renounced life, Buddha remarked:

> Two kinds of happiness exist: one in lay life [*gihi sukha*] and the other in renounced life [*pabbajja sukha*]. Of these two, happiness in renounced life is better.
> Two kinds of happiness exist: one derived from sensory satisfaction [*kama sukha*] and the other derived from giving up sensory satisfaction [*nekkhamma sukha*]. Of these two, the happiness derived from giving up sensory satisfaction is better.[2]

These two utterances offer a vital clue to understanding Buddha's attitude toward happiness in lay life. He explicitly noted that happiness exists in lay life and in the satisfaction of the senses. Even in the presence of Bhikkhus who needed strong emphasis on the dissatisfaction of secular life, Buddha never denied happiness in the material and sensory world. He merely placed happiness in the renounced life above happiness in lay life. In other words, Buddha proclaimed that happiness in secular life is not a fallacy or a myth, but a reality.

More evidence found elsewhere in the *Sutta Pitaka* confirms Buddha's attitude. While defining happiness, Buddha again said:

> Happiness exists in worldly life . . . What is that happiness? It is the satisfaction gained through the five senses [*kamaguna*]. Sensory objects related to sight, sound, smell, taste, and physical contact do exist. These objects are attractive, desirable, pleasant, appealing, and worthy. Experiences through the five senses mean the fivefold advantage one can obtain in lay life. The happiness one derives from experiencing these five kinds of benefits is called happiness in worldly life.[3]

Buddha's view that happiness exists in secular life is clear and complete. A layperson constantly undergoes pleasant sensory experiences, which Buddha called *kamaguna*. Altogether, one can obtain five such benefits: beautiful visual objects, pleasing sounds, pleasant scent, delicious taste, and agreeable physical contact. These benefits are inherent in worldly life, and people are entitled to make themselves happy by experiencing them. Clearly, Buddha accepted worldly happiness as a true experience in lay life.

Buddha's appreciation of lay life

Not only did Buddha admit the existence of happiness in secular life, but he also admired both secular life itself and the happiness therein. As previously mentioned, Buddha stressed that happiness in lay life is secondary to happiness in renounced life. However, this assertion does not mean a devaluation of a layperson's life. Instead, it means that a more profound happiness awaits those who are willing to give up worldly pleasure. That happiness, called *vimutti sukha* or "happiness in detachment," was experienced by Buddha himself and by his ordained disciples.

Buddha emphasized that happiness in renounced life would be better because renunciation would grant a stable form of happiness. With fewer duties, those who renounce worldly life would find fewer hindrances to their inner peace. Happiness in lay life, on the other hand, would fluctuate constantly because of the numerous conflicts and burdens that are inherent in that life. Other than this comparison, which raised spiritual happiness above worldly happiness, no evidence suggests that Buddha found fault with secular life or the happiness associated with it.

Buddha's guidance of lay life

Since Buddha appreciated lay life, he readily advised and instructed people who were interested in knowing more about how to make their lives happier and more prosperous. Many people visited Buddha and requested guidance toward success and happiness. The following request, which occurs in many Suttas, echoes what the lay community expected from Buddha:

> Master, we are the laypeople who live with a family, wear beautiful clothes, use perfumes and ornaments, and accept gold and silver. Please advise us in such a way that we may make our present existence and the next life happy.[4]

In reply to these requests, Buddha never showed the slightest disrespect for the speaker's style of living. Instead, he often went on to give detailed explanations on how to make the listener's life more successful. He identified these instructions as *sampada*, the factors that would bring benefits for secular life. Forty-five years of his vigorous social involvement left invaluable pieces of such instructions in the *Sutta Pitaka*.

Why Buddha emphasized the concept of dissatisfaction in worldly life

Despite Buddha's considerable attention to the layperson's happiness and material success, we need to admit that the *Sutta Pitaka* also contains passages with seemingly conflicting views. We find that some of Buddha's speeches advocate the concepts of dissatisfaction in the material world, as well as mental detachment from worldly pleasure. These concepts, which occur repeatedly in numerous Suttas, present a contradictory view about Buddha's teaching.

Nevertheless, we need to look at these discourses from a social and historical point of view in order to discover their audience and purpose. Particularly, confusion about Buddha's different audiences has led to the misinterpretation of his teaching.

As noted above, Buddha spent considerable time striving to counter the concepts presented by some traditionalists and extremist groups. For this purpose, he needed a committed and accomplished community. The Vedic system had Brahmins, the educated ascetics, who defiantly defended its tradition. The Jain Order had already trained its own male and female ascetics to organize its social system. Influenced by both traditions, Buddha molded the concept of Sangha, the ordained community, to fulfill an important need—that of organizing a highly dedicated and qualified community to take his message to society. The concepts of impermanence and dissatisfaction with worldly pleasure, and detachment from secular life predominantly served the purpose of training and maintaining the community of Sangha.

This statement does not suggest that Nibbana, the blissful state that one can achieve by eliminating mental attachment to worldly pleasure, is merely a technique to train the Sangha. We can hardly disregard Buddha's and his disciples' repeated assertion that their detached existence was extremely happy. Irrespective of time and place, one may still experience the same happiness if one begins to detach oneself from the greedy pursuit of sensory pleasures.

At the same time, the concept of detachment from worldly pleasure also served as an effective technique to train, organize, and strengthen the community of monks and nuns, the very foundation that stabilized Buddha's position in society. The repeated emphasis on mental suffering in the material world was meant for that community and for those who were interested in entering it. The same teaching was not relevant to Buddha's lay community.

Mental detachment from sensual pleasure seems to have provided a dependable cause for Buddha's ordained community to live a renounced life. A modern-day priest would prefer a spiritual life simply in order to serve a divine power. However, such a religious motive was hardly present in Buddha's teaching. Buddha encouraged men and women to enter the community of Sangha because he knew that renounced life would allow for more inner peace than would lay life. He encouraged these disciples to meditate constantly on the impermanence and dissatisfaction of worldly pleasure. He guided them to change their attitudes toward secular life. This attitudinal change made Buddha's ordained disciples well-controlled and dedicated monks and nuns who successfully promoted the social influence Buddha intended.

Buddha's different audiences

We need to identify Buddha's audience for certain discourses instead of embracing a misleading claim that everything in the *Sutta Pitaka* is for everybody. Just because Buddha repeatedly told his ordained disciples to meditate on impermanence and dissatisfaction, we cannot conclude that Buddha wanted everybody to follow that teaching. In fact, the *Nikayas*, the collections of Buddha's most authentic speeches, do not provide evidence of his appeal to his lay followers to meditate on impermanence or dissatisfaction. Buddha, of course, recommended useful meditation methods for his lay community, but they were never meant to obstruct happiness in lay life. Instead, original texts show that Buddha persuaded his lay disciples to live their lives joyfully and meaningfully.

Considering the purpose and the audience of Suttas, we may roughly categorize them into three divisions:

1. Instructive discourses for the ordained and soon-to-be-ordained disciples
2. Rational and argumentative speeches to counter opposing views
3. Instructive and rational discourses for the lay community

Of these three groups, the Suttas that addressed the ordained community of males (Bhikkhus) clearly outnumber other Suttas. This fact may lead to the erroneous conclusion that Buddha's whole endeavor was to train his Bhikkhus, not to help his lay followers. Nevertheless, the overload of these Suttas in the *Sutta Pitaka* seems to be a result of some reasons other than Buddha's overwhelming attention to Bhikkhus alone.

Why Buddha's teaching for lay life appeared less important in the *Sutta Pitaka*

We must step into history in order to provide a clear answer to this question. What is important is to find out who preserved Buddha's speeches, and how, for nearly twenty-six centuries. Information gathered in this search will provide the answer to why Buddha's guidance of the layperson never occupied its due position in the *Sutta Pitaka*.

First, those who preserved Buddha's speeches were the Bhikkhus, who considered Buddha's instructions for themselves most important. Over 80 percent of all Suttas in the *Sutta Pitaka* are addressed to Bhikkhus and contain instructions for them. Even though Buddha traveled continuously for forty-five years and talked to a great multitude of people, only a very small percentage of such speeches seems to have been recorded. In contrast, we find in the *Sutta Pitaka* a continuous repetition of instructions Buddha had given to Bhikkhus inside a monastery. Seemingly, Bhikkhus were more interested in preserving what they found useful for themselves, not what Buddha taught the public.

From the Bhikkhus' point of view, such a partial preservation of Buddha's teaching is understandable. Immediately after Buddha's death, senior Bhikkhus found that their most urgent need was to retain unity and discipline among themselves. With their community expanding, different views and practices emerged from within and demanded action. The first major council, held just three months after Buddha passed away, was partly prompted by the unruly behavior of some Bhikkhus. Repeated emphasis of Buddha's advice to Bhikkhus was urgent in this situation. The ordained disciples, who memorized Pali Suttas for preservation, seem to have added, modified, and dropped many Suttas in order to stress the disciplines for their own community.

This approach, however, altered the overall outlook of Buddha's teaching. In the preserved *Sutta Pitaka*, Buddha's instructions for Bhikkhus seemed more prominent and the guidance of his lay community more obscure. Consequently, a reader of the *Sutta Pitaka* might assume that Buddha ignored his lay disciples.

The method of grouping the Suttas has also made Buddha's speeches for the lay community appear less important. At the first Sangha council, many Suttas were categorized according to their length. For instance, Buddha's long dialogues were grouped in the *Digha Nikaya*, literally "the section of long discourses." Hundreds of shorter Suttas were placed in the *Majjhima Nikaya*, the section for middle-length sayings. Thousands of other Suttas were arranged in the *Anguttara Nikaya* according to a numerical order. For example, any of Buddha's speeches that explained two causes, two effects, two kinds of individuals, and so on were grouped under Number Two. Sub-numerical headings were also added to further organize the division. Clearly, the categorization of Buddha's discourses was based on their external appearance, not on the value of their content. As a result, we find Buddha's speeches for the lay community thinly scattered throughout the *Sutta Pitaka*.

In addition, most of the Suttas related to lay life were separated from similar Suttas and placed among hundreds of Suttas intended for the ordained disciples. This arrangement again presents Buddha's advice for lay life as insignificant and contradictory. A modern reader may still believe that the recurring concept of dissatisfaction is Buddha's philosophy for everyone's life.

Recent misinterpretations

In fact, some writers and translators in recent history have been caught in this confusion and have thought, mistakenly, that the path Buddha recommended for his ordained disciples was his teaching for everyone. Such concepts as Buddhist pessimism and suffering emerged in the aftermath of that misunderstanding. Reportedly, Arthur Schopenhauer, the renowned German thinker, formed his theory of pessimism after reading the few Buddhist texts that were available to him in translation. He expressed his appreciation of Buddha, paving the way for critics to compare his philosophy to Buddha's. As a result, the term "Buddhist pessimism," along with Schopenhauer's theory of pessimism, earned recognition in the Western world.

Further, almost every translator of Suttas rendered the recurrent keyword *dukkha* as "suffering," and had readers believe that Buddha regarded worldly life as miserable. However, *dukkha* indicates the insatiable nature of the human mind, not so-called suffering. Buddha employed this word for the purpose of directing the Bhikkhus toward Nibbana, not for the instruction of his lay disciples. Worst of all, hundreds of books written about Buddha's teaching have identified his instructions for the ordained community as the central teaching for the entire Buddhist community. This misconception has led to the common assumption that Buddha discounted worldly life and scorned its happiness.

An effort to uncover the truth

Closer attention to the *Sutta Pitaka* would make it clear that Buddha's teaching for the layperson is more secular than most people expect it to be. Altogether, we find in the *Sutta Pitaka* more than one hundred discourses, ranging from long dialogues to short utterances, dealing exclusively with lay life. The following chapters will focus on these Suttas in order to clarify Buddha's attitude toward worldly life and to elucidate his guidance of the layperson toward success and happiness.

Chapter Two

....

Freedom to Be Prosperous

Poverty is a cause of pain for lay-people. Being poor, they run into debt. This situation would lead them into a decline.

Buddha, the *Gradual Sayings*

Buddha's approach to prosperity stands out as one of the most misinterpreted aspects of his teaching. Many writers have either stated or implied that Buddha did not encourage people to prosper and become wealthy. Influenced by this misinterpretation, some tend to believe that to achieve prosperity means to go against Buddha. As we have already discussed the reasons for these misinterpretations and misconceptions, further elaboration seems unnecessary at this point. With the main focus on Buddha's speeches, let us examine the attitude he actually maintained with regard to the layperson's wealth and prosperity.

First, Buddha never imposed limitations on the layperson's effort to be successful. Instead, he clearly encouraged his lay followers to strive for success. Whether the occupation is "trading, cattle farming, archery, government service, or any other profession or industry," the layperson should strive to advance in his or her respective field.[1] Notably, the motivation to achieve success is an important requirement in any person's life. An attitude such as "I have a job, and it is enough for me to live" has no place in Buddha's teaching.

Next, Buddha saw no limits to the amount of a layperson's wealth. He never told any of his prosperous lay followers to stop or slow down their efforts to be wealthier. Instead, he unequivocally encouraged the lay community to plan, organize, and endeavor to obtain more. We will discuss these instructions in detail in later chapters, but the fact that needs emphasis at this point is that Buddha enforced no restrictions on the personal wealth of the layperson. *Ulare bhoge* (immense wealth)[2] was the phrase he used to measure the quantity of wealth that an individual could amass. This phrase indicates that a person may strive to be as wealthy as possible.

Conditional freedom to gain prosperity

What is important, however, is that the freedom Buddha offered to the individual to be as prosperous as possible hinges on two conditions. First, the individual must follow certain guidelines during his or her endeavor to be prosperous. Second, he or she must use wealth in the proper way. The enormous wealth one might acquire would never be subject to Buddha's praise unless these two conditions are met. So, on the one hand, the boundless freedom Buddha gave the layperson to be wealthy relates to the quantity of wealth, not to the means of its accumulation. On the other hand, prosperity itself should be not an end, but merely a means to a wholesome purpose.

The following words of Buddha denote both the individual freedom to be prosperous and the importance of using that freedom correctly:

> What is *atthi sukha* [the happiness of possessing wealth]? A certain person accumulates great wealth and property through fair means and right effort and thinks, "Now I have wealth; now I have property gathered through fair means." In thinking so, that person experiences happiness and satisfaction. This is what I call *atthi sukha*.[3]

So, he clearly supported individual prosperity if the layperson employed "fair means and right effort" to be prosperous. In fact, huge wealth accumulated through fair means is a source of great happiness for the layperson. In various speeches, Buddha explained in detail what he meant by the term "fair means and right effort," but first let us have a look at his contemporaries' views about the means of increasing wealth. They will provide a clear background for understanding what Buddha actually meant by "fair means and right effort."

Some of the teachers contemporary with Buddha argued that respect for ethical values would be unimportant in one's effort to be prosperous. They advised people, including the mighty king Ajatasattu, that one could gather wealth through whatever means necessary.[4] One should not worry about how harmful the means would be to others. For instance, Kassapa, one of the famous teachers during Buddha's time, found no fault with stealing and housebreaking.[5] Other materialists such as Ajita and Kaccayana held similar views. They blatantly disregarded the ethics involved in one's effort to be prosperous.

The Carvaka tradition, another famous Indian materialistic school of thought during the sixth century B.C., summed up the easiest means of achieving wealth: "Borrow throughout life and enjoy with no intention to pay back."

Buddha's honorable path to prosperity

Buddha's advocacy of an honorable path to prosperity can be evaluated in the light of the materialistic views discussed above. He introduced a system of ethics into the process of acquiring wealth. On the one hand, his general ethics, which always advocated compassion for others, are certainly applicable to the individual's endeavor to achieve wealth. In addition, Buddha also set some specific guidelines regarding business ethics.

First, the person who is engaged in profit making should not deceive or hurt the customers or any other persons involved. He or she must "gradually increase wealth without squeezing others just as bees collect honey without harming flowers."[6] Whatever wealth one possesses should have been acquired "through just means."[7] Fairness is so vital to one's effort to make a profit that, before beginning an ambitious profession or business, one should first make a resolution not to exploit others.

Buddha's recommendations for the welfare of employees further clarify the honorable path he introduced for the layperson's material success. He specifically mentioned that an employer should treat workers in the following five ways:

1. Assign work and duties in accordance with their skill and ability.

2. Pay a salary befitting their work and service.

3. Provide medical assistance.

4. Make wholesome food available.

5. Allow leave and vacations at the right time.[8]

These amazingly modern concepts confirm Buddha's teaching that people are not entitled to wealth if they fail to follow ethical business practices. Employers should refrain from forcing hard labor on others and should pay a suitable salary to their employees. Providing workers with medical care, food, and leave is an important requirement in any profit-making endeavor. These points make it clear that, from Buddha's viewpoint, those who fail to provide welfare for their workers are unqualified to be wealthy.

Overall, Buddha reminded ambitious people that they should be mindful about their ethics regarding both customers and employees. Leaders in the business field need to satisfy their customers and also to protect the rights and privileges of their employees. As long as people follow these steps, they are at least partially qualified to become more prosperous.

How to use wealth effectively

Proper use of wealth, the other qualification for prosperity, can also be clarified in the light of how some thinkers contemporary with Buddha wanted their listeners to use wealth. These "teachers" taught that one's own sensory satisfaction is the most important purpose of having wealth. According to their way of thinking, one should use every possible means to gratify one's senses as long as one lives. In this context, charity makes no sense at all. Buddha held a different view. He emphasized that the wealth one acquires through just means should be used for the benefit of others in addition to oneself:

> The layperson who acquires immense wealth with effort, skill,

hard work, and respect for justice uses it [wealth] to satisfy his
or her own senses and to please himself or herself. Using wealth,
he or she experiences happiness in life. At the same time, that
person makes his or her parents, family [husband or wife and
children], and employees happy and satisfied.
Second, the wealthy person uses his or her wealth to treat
friends and associates.
Again, the wealthy person uses his or her wealth to please relatives and the needy [atithi], to honor dead relatives, to fulfill duties to the government, and to conduct rituals.
Finally, the wealthy person uses his or her wealth to feed
those Bhikkhus and Brahmins who have dedicated their lives
to self-purification and realization of enlightenment.[9]

Behind its apparent social and historical outlook, this quotation il-
lustrates Buddha's basic view about how one should use one's wealth.
While wealth is primarily for the fulfillment of individual needs and
self-comfort, it is also for providing comfort and satisfaction for a
host of others, including family members, friends, employees, and
the needy. Buddha repeatedly emphasized that human effort should
be meaningful to the person who makes such an effort and to those
who live with that person or, broadly speaking, to the whole of society.
"Proper use of wealth" can be defined as an exemplification of this
central teaching of Buddha.

Those who failed to use their wealth in this balanced way fell short
of Buddha's admiration. King Kosala told Buddha that he (the king)
had just taken over the huge wealth of a merchant who had died without an heir. The value of the merchant's gold alone was eight hundred
thousand, but he had always worn rags, eaten cheap rice, and traveled in a small, shabby caravan. Also, he had never used his wealth for
others' welfare. Buddha said in response that one who would fail to
use wealth for one's own benefit and for that of others would not live a
meaningful life.[10]

In contrast, those who used their wealth to benefit themselves and
others won Buddha's great appreciation. Similar to "a rainfall that

nourishes life," great individual wealth should foster a host of people.[11] Essentially, "proper use" is the objective of having wealth. Buddha indicated that, as long as one follows guidance for the use of wealth, one is entitled to make every effort to earn more.

The *Sutta Pitaka* provides no evidence of what percentage of wealth one should allocate for one's own use, for one's children, and for others. Nevertheless, advising business people, Buddha suggested that one may divide one's income into four equal portions. Two portions should be invested, one should be saved, and the remaining portion could be taken for living expenses.[12] This suggestion indicates that Buddha did not want people to let their holdings dwindle away by mere spending and giving. He regarded savings as essential because "savings can be used in the event of an unexpected tragedy or misfortune."[13] When Buddha recommended one of four equal portions of income for use, he apparently included in it all expenditure such as personal expenses and donations. In other words, one can make oneself and others happy with only a certain portion of one's wealth, not with everything one earns.

The quotation cited above also recognized that taking care of children, protecting the rights of employees, and paying a portion of personal income to the government are essential components of proper use of wealth. Those who do not follow these practices do not deserve to be more prosperous. As Buddha observed, the fulfillment of one's duties toward society is an important practice for the layperson. Allocation of a portion of one's assets for society would be a demonstration of that practice.

An important verse in *Parabhava Sutta* sheds more light on Buddha's emphasis that one's own wealth is not merely for oneself. Citing the signs of a layperson's degeneration, Buddha said:

> If one who possesses wealth, much gold, and food uses them for oneself, one is on the way to downfall.[14]

This statement confirms Buddha's disapproval of a wealthy person's disregard for society. "Using for oneself" may mean both one's own personal use of wealth and its use by family members alone. Since people are certainly indebted to society for their own prosperity, they are obliged to contribute to society instead of using their wealth for themselves.

Another question that awaits clarification at this point is how, and to what extent, one may satisfy one's own senses with the wealth garnered through just means. Some may boldly assume that they are entitled to satisfy their senses freely if they earn wealth through fair means, and use a part of it for others. However, this conclusion clearly contradicts Buddha's teaching about the owner's personal use of his or her wealth.

Buddha never promoted a *carpe diem* theory, the belief that sensory satisfaction is the purpose of having wealth. Instead, he admired the person who "acquires immense wealth but is not intoxicated by it."[15] Buddha remarked that those who exceed the limits of sensory satisfaction would "suffer later from the related adverse effects."[16] One must be aware of the right measure of sensory gratification, the measure that would ultimately lead to physical well-being and long life.

Buddha's advice to King Kosala about overeating confirms this conclusion. The king, well known for his huge belly, was an ardent pleasure-seeker, particularly where food and drink were concerned. He possessed an easygoing personality and developed a close friendship with Buddha. Once, immediately after having a huge meal, he visited Buddha, panting and in visible discomfort. After observing the king's situation, Buddha uttered a stanza which praised eating in right measure. He stated that such a person—one who knows the right measure of food—would get rid of physical discomfort and enjoy a long, healthy life.[17] These words are applicable to the enjoyment of any form of sensual pleasure. "Right measure" is the key phrase. Right measure keeps the individual within the zone of physical comfort and health, mental well-being, and social acceptance.

Summary

Buddha elaborated his views on how people should feel about their wealth, and guided them toward gaining the proper advantages from their wealth. He stressed that wealth is a clear source of happiness for laypersons. However, to achieve that happiness, they need to earn wealth in the right way and use it in the most effective way. Money or wealth is neither to keep nor to use solely for one's own sensory satisfaction, but to make oneself and others happy and satisfied. While using wealth for oneself, one should be aware of the right measure of sensory satisfaction. Prosperity, according to Buddha, is a reward when the prosperous follow his recommended guidelines.

Chapter Three

Path to Prosperity

I found out two important principles: not to be content with what I had achieved and not to give up the effort for the highest achievement.

Right effort is the first step toward success. Right effort brings benefits and happiness to a layperson.

Buddha, the *Gradual Sayings*

While praising prosperity as an accomplishment for a layperson, Buddha volunteered to guide his lay followers toward material success. In this undertaking, he discussed a wide range of topics that introduced and elaborated on the requirements for the initiation and continuation of an ambitious effort. Buddha's guidance of the layperson's material success is a complete and thoroughly effective process. Focusing on his instructions on how to launch a successful effort, this chapter will open the discussion of his guidance of the layperson's material success.

Inner preparation: the initial prerequisite

According to Buddha's observation, inner preparation represents one of the most important prerequisites for any kind of success. He seemingly recommended the same preparation for a layperson's journey toward prosperity. First, he advocated the removal of psychological barriers that would obstruct a person's progress. Next, he clarified how right attitude would inject power into a person's endeavor. Overall, Buddha indicated that psychological preparation is a crucial factor for a person's material success. The following two steps explain the basic requirements for inner preparation:

1. Remove the inner barriers

Self-imposed limitations, as Buddha interpreted them, are the biggest hindrance to individual progress in either spiritual or secular life. These limitations signify the devaluation of one's own capabilities, skills, and potential. Buddha identified society as the breeding ground of this low mentality. Social doctrines that blatantly undermine human potential would invade the mind and eventually overpower it. Buddha advised his lay followers to ignore such views and to rely on their own potential in order to facilitate the elimination of these barriers.

For a better understanding of Buddha's message, we may look at
some views present in his society. These views devalued individual
ability and prevented people's progress in material life. For instance,
his society held that a person born into the Shudra caste should not
make any effort to do business. A Shudra's predestined occupation
was believed to be the performance of servile duties for people of other
castes. Similarly, only a Brahmin was permitted to become a spiritual
leader. Not even a member of the ruling caste could do so because
Brahma, the creator, had allegedly assigned that task to the Brahmin
caste only.

Buddha vehemently opposed such views. He argued convincingly
that intention and right effort—not any form of predetermination—
would serve as an essential foundation for material success. First, he
explored, analyzed, and rationally refuted the views of his contemporaries that advocated predetermination of the individual's degree
of happiness or suffering. Altogether, he found three such views: the
will of Brahma, the Vedic theory of Karma, and the universal law of
predetermination.[1]

Those who attributed human progress or downfall to the will of
Brahma maintained that higher social positions and various professions were decided by Brahma on the basis of caste. They alleged that
society should, therefore, desist from making any changes to the prevalent social law. The advocates of the Karma theory asserted that
one's happiness and sorrow were solely decided by one's actions in past
lives. This teaching also denied human effort. The third theory asserted that whatever was to happen would happen despite one's effort to
change it. This theory was based on the determinist view that every
individual, whether saint or villain, would exist for a definite number
of births before total cessation.

From Buddha's standpoint, all three views were extremist theories
that would invalidate human will and effort to succeed.[2] His argumentation was strong and rational. He claimed that the theorists who held

the views mentioned above could not expect any spiritual progress for themselves. Meditation and other such preferred methods would fail to purify them because effort had no value within the teaching of these theorists. Buddha would address them and say, "You have denied human need and human effort to change."[3]

His denial of these extremist views had one specific aim: removal of the inner barriers that hampered his followers' progress either in spiritual or material success. Buddha's message to his lay disciples was that they should not live in inner cages, thereby imprisoning their potential. By shattering these barriers, they would prepare themselves for a promising future.

2. Have faith in your own potential

After helping his lay followers to eliminate their inner obstructions, Buddha guided them toward self-reliance, the next step in laying the foundation for a successful future. As mentioned in this chapter, Buddha lived in an era in which individual strength had clearly been denied. He saw no other factor than self-reliance to prepare an individual for any kind of success.

Buddha's life itself provides a prime example of his strong position in this regard. As discussed above, some teachers during his time adhered to the widespread, firmly held belief that Brahma allowed only members of the Brahmin caste to become spiritual leaders. However, Buddha, who belonged to the ruling caste, demonstrated the fallacy of this view by becoming one of the most successful spiritual teachers who ever lived. He achieved that success with unshakable self-confidence. The following utterance at the time of his preparation for his eventual liberation is a clear example of his determination:

> Let my flesh and blood dry up, leaving my skin, veins, and bones. Still, I shall not give up my effort until I achieve the highest level which can be won by human ability, human effort, and human action.[4]

This attitude eventually strengthened Buddha's mind for the final conquest of greed (*lobha*), malice (*dosa*), and illusion (*moha*). He attained enlightenment, or the highest level of inner purification, with the development of unsurpassable wisdom and boundless feelings of generosity and compassion. Having sat under a Bo tree one night with firm determination, he continued with meditation and stood up in the morning victorious and self-contented.

While talking to the ordained disciples about their spiritual success and encouraging his lay disciples toward material success, Buddha emphasized the same initial preparation: empowerment of mind with firm determination. The sentence "I can do it if I follow the right path" exemplifies Buddha's motto for the person who is brimming with aspirations.

Planned effort: the perfect beginning

The two steps discussed above—removal of inner barriers and enhancement of the mind with self-reliance—set the stage for the layperson's inner preparation for success. Next comes the planned effort, which signals the perfect beginning of any successful endeavor. Having cleansed his or her mind of fear and doubt, now the person can get into the real work with unsurpassed confidence.

Two characteristics of effort, as Buddha identified them, are worth mentioning at this point. First, effort alone makes inner preparation meaningful. In other words, in the absence of effort, inner preparation is certainly inadequate for success. Buddha never promoted such views as "Visualize it and wait; you will get it." Instead, he asserted that the right effort should definitely follow the right thought. Buddha's message is: "You can succeed if you pursue your goal with confidence." Individual effort, according to his teaching, plays a predominant role in making a person successful in his or her secular life.

Next, effort means more than mere hard work. Buddha did not

offer a simple philosophy such as "Work hard and achieve success." Instead, he emphasized that the layperson needs to strive wisely and methodically in order to achieve success. According to Buddha's observation, wise decisions and wise actions, rather than mere hard work, would make the layperson's effort genuinely meaningful.

Buddha introduced four steps for his lay disciples to reap the best results from effort. He explained right effort as follows:

> What is the right effort [to succeed in secular life]? Suppose a certain person maintained his or her life with trading, cattle-farming, archery, government service, or any other profession or industry. That person develops knowledge and skills in the profession, acquires organizational skills, does the necessary work at the right time, and shows strategic search for new means of improvement. This is what I call the right effort.[5]

Despite its brevity, possibly caused by the Bhikkhus' summarization of a long speech for the sake of preservation through memory, this definition of right effort is thorough by any standard. Notably, Buddha indicated that wise decisions and right actions combine together to lead an individual toward success. The four steps Buddha recommended in this passage are so important that each of them deserves a detailed discussion.

Step 1: Develop knowledge and skills in the desired profession or business

Acquisition of knowledge and various skills in the relevant field highlights an essential part of right effort. The Pali term Buddha used in this context is *dakkho alam katum*, which means "improvement of abilities necessary for doing the work." *Dakkho* includes both knowledge and skill. These qualities provide a person with proficiency in his or her professional field. Consequently, the layperson learns to excel in what is undertaken. A trader, for instance, may develop a thorough knowledge about what he buys from the wholesale market, be aware of his resale profits, and be skillful in buying and selling.[6] Overall, one needs to possess considerable knowledge and skill in the relevant field in order to strive correctly.

This improvement is a process which should be initiated by parents during their offspring's childhood. In *Sigalovada Sutta*, Buddha noted that parents should take the initial responsibility for guiding their children toward a suitable profession.[7] As a child enters adulthood, he or she would take the responsibility for further enhancement of knowledge and skill.

In the modern context, education, job-related training, and business-related research and studies are all different aspects of the same requirement. We are well aware that success in this competitive world depends on qualifications. Those who enjoy commanding positions in the modern workforce are the people who have gained masterly knowledge and developed superb skills. They are also the ones who rapidly and steadily advance in business. This truth proves Buddha's point that education and skill development are essential components for those who strive for success.

A modern psychologist would identify this level of improvement as the self-actualized stage in skill development. The majority of people in any society acquire only basic knowledge and skills in various positions. A small percentage, however, go beyond that level; they develop specialized knowledge and skills in their respective fields. Buddha wanted his lay followers to actualize themselves in their professions. So, he recommended better knowledge and skill as being indispensable to initiate the march toward material success.

Step 2: Organize work and business skillfully

Organizational skills constitute another significant prerequisite for the person who strives to advance in his or her selected field. Buddha consistently emphasized the importance of organizing one's work and business. In *Mangala Sutta*, he stated that "having organized work and business" is a blessing to the layperson.[8] The Pali term he used to mean "organizational skill" is *dakkho alam sanvidhatum* (becoming genuinely skillful in organization).

Of course, organizational skill is a broad topic in Buddha's speeches. This skill includes both self-organization and work-related organization. Again, organizational skill is useful for both the initiation and the successful continuation of any task. In this section of the book, we will pay close attention to the skills that are particularly important for organizing the initial phase of an ambitious project. The same skills may also be applied at other stages of work and business.

Buddha's own biography provides clear evidence of what he meant by organizational skill. After reaching the highest level of inner purification, Buddha launched one of the most successful humanistic projects ever recorded in history. He initiated a massive program to influence social thinking in order to bring about social changes. One of the first steps he took for this purpose was organization.

Initially, Buddha organized himself. His daily routine indicates how organized he was. He divided his daily activities into five sessions.[9] The first was the early morning session, which he used for his own meditation practices. Then, he allocated the morning session for visits to people who needed his help. During the afternoon session, he instructed his ordained disciples and any lay followers who visited him. Two night sessions were used for the guidance of ordained disciples' meditation practices and for the discussion of profound Dhamma topics. Buddha organized his energetic life in the most systematic way.

Buddha also demonstrated amazing skills in organizing the new society he had established. He was the first social reformer to bring such a systematic order to a social movement. First, he appointed Sariputta and Moggallana, two of his most qualified ordained disciples, as his chief leaders. Then, he offered titles to eighty Bhikkhus and assigned them positions of leadership based on their knowledge and skill in their respective fields. Through his own leadership, Buddha demonstrated how an organized effort would lead a person to amazing success.

In his advice to lay followers, organization of the workforce drew Buddha's special attention. He specifically mentioned that qualified persons should be appointed as leaders. "Giving leadership to a woman or a man who follows addictive habits and squanders wealth signifies decline," Buddha remarked.[10] Also, as mentioned in the previous chapter, the leadership should assign the employees work and duties that would fit their skills and abilities. In addition, the employer should offer benefits, leaves of absence, and food to the employees. These steps also indicate the organization of the workforce.

This approach would also contribute to the success of the business in a different way. Especially, the employees, thus treated, would develop a very favorable attitude toward the employer. Consequently, they would work to the best of their capabilities. "Commitment to the job, refraining from wrongdoing such as stealing, and appreciation of the employer" are some of the favorable results that may be obtained by satisfying the workers.[11] Such a reaction from the workers would definitely contribute to the success of any business.

Buddha also discussed how to organize a small business such as home production of clothes made of cotton or wool, a widespread occupation during his time. He regarded that type of small business as family work, in which both husband and wife should share responsibilities. Interestingly, the wife should be in charge of organizing a family-based cotton or wool business,[12] an idea that highlights Buddha's high regard of women's skill and intellectual strength.

Overall, Buddha guided his ambitious lay followers to stay on a systematic and organized course of action in order to achieve their objectives. This guidance is evident from both his life and his teaching. He organized his actions and plans, indirectly citing himself as an example to follow. Moreover, he offered his lay followers invaluable instructions on how to organize their work and businesses.

Step 3: Complete the necessary tasks at the right time

Timely action, from Buddha's point of view, is one of the most crucial factors for his lay followers' success. This requirement, of course, may relate to organization, but Buddha identified timely action separately because of its overwhelming importance in any endeavor. While he was talking to King Kosala, Buddha cited timing as the single most important factor for a person's success in material life:

> The most important factor for a person's development is doing the action at the right time. A footprint of an elephant can cover the footprint of any walking animal. Similarly, in its importance, timely action stands out among all other actions.[13]

This statement pinpoints the importance of timing. Buddha asserted that the layperson who strives for success should essentially do the right actions at the right time. He warned that one who fails to act at the right time would also "fail to acquire new wealth, and what one has already acquired will soon diminish."[14] Buddha used such words as *analasa* and *appamada* to represent this overwhelmingly important requirement for achievement.

Existent English translations, however, fail to convey the broad meanings embodied in these original Pali words. *Analasa* is generally translated as "not being lazy" while *appamada* is interpreted as "heedfulness" or "diligence." Literally, these translations are acceptable, but they simply point to hard work as a means to success. As Buddha used them, however, these Pali words carry a more profound meaning: they emphasize the importance of right action at the right time.

The "action" may be a laborious task that demands both physical and mental energy, or it (action) may be just a decision or a step that needs a few minutes of thinking. Regardless, the layperson who is striving for success should take action at the proper time.

Taking examples from everyday life, Buddha explained that some people would lazily avoid and postpone work, blaming weather, citing hunger or fullness, or saying that it would be too early or too late for work.[15] These examples show that the opposite of *analasa* is negligence, procrastination, or lethargic postponement of work, a dangerous habit that clearly thwarts one's effort for success. Thus, *analasa* signifies the use of physical energy at the right time.

In his conversation with King Kosala, Buddha used the word *ap-pamada* to mean "timely action."[16] "If you live your life doing the right action without delay, you protect and save yourself, your elephants, your wealth, and your storehouses," he remarked.[17] Buddha also mentioned in the same speech that King Kosala's timely actions would encourage his staff and employees to perform their own duties on time. These remarks suggest that timely action in this context means taking the right steps and making decisions accordingly, rather than doing arduous work.

In general, well-timed actions, from Buddha's perspective, make a layperson's endeavor for success profoundly meaningful. Those who fail to time their actions properly in their effort to earn wealth would resemble "a weak heron near a dry pond."[18] Citing this example, Buddha strove to encourage his followers to act at the most appropriate time.

Step 4: Look for strategic means of improvement

Vyagghapajja Sutta concluded Buddha's definition of the layperson's effort for success by citing the search for strategic means of improvement. This step may be regarded as one of the most innovative and effective practices to lead an individual toward success. In brief, this approach means the introduction of new concepts into the professional and business fields, and the application of new methods to improve overall performance.

The relevant Pali term is *upaya vimamsa*, a technical phrase that has drawn hardly any attention. *Upaya* means "strategic approach," or "thinking out of the box," as opposed to the commonly accepted way of trying something. *Vimamsa* has several meanings, such as "examination" and "testing." Taken together as a technique for one's effort to succeed in lay life, *upaya vimamsa* means "strategic investigation of new means of improvement in the professional and business field."

This technique may very well be called innovation, as opposed to the following of tradition. Buddha would have been aware of new developments in his society, particularly in the fields of business and trading. As noted in Chapter One, the sixth century B.C. was the emerging age of business in India, with altogether new innovations. Hundreds of carts from the states of Magadha and Kosala took merchandise to Gandhara to be transported to the Greek islands. Goods also reached Barygaza, a port on the Western coast of India, to be transported to the Western world via the Red Sea. In these ventures, new strategies had to be implemented in order to protect, transport, sell, and exchange merchandise.

For instance, Buddha's chief supporter Anathapindika, a business tycoon in Savatthi, had formed a trade organization to collect and export merchandise to the Western world. Upali, another supporter of Buddha, had begun the first known banking system. Buddha's awareness of these new developments in trading and business may have persuaded him to encourage his lay followers to implement new methods for their material success.

Whatever the reason, Buddha offered an invaluable piece of advice to his motivated lay followers: "Invent new concepts and strategies to steer your journey toward success." He himself practiced the same philosophy when he established and organized his new society within the traditional rigid society. He achieved exceptional success in his own endeavor, demonstrating the superiority of this concept.

Summary

Buddha offered useful instructions to guide his lay followers' initial effort for prosperity. He first shaped their mentality and strengthened their mind. Next, he guided their effort, offering useful instructions to make it truly meaningful. Buddha did not encourage his lay community to wait for a sudden fortune, such as a modern lottery win. Neither did he tolerate quick and easy money through whatever means. Instead, he helped his disciples to strive methodically and to establish themselves in life "just as ants build up their anthill."[19]

New knowledge and the development of skills, organization, timely action, and innovative methods constitute the right effort for success, according to Buddha.

Chapter Four
Nine Steps to Retain Prosperity

The layperson's objective, "I should live a long and dignified life with my relatives and teachers with the wealth obtained through rightful means," is pleasant, agreeable, charming, and only achievable through effort.

Buddha, the *Gradual Sayings*

Buddha observed two kinds of people: those who attained prosperity but failed to retain it, and those who became prosperous and secured their prosperity. "Some families obtain great wealth, but cannot hold on to it for long," he stated.[1] In the same Sutta, he mentioned that other families kept their prosperity undiminished. Buddha examined why and how some succeeded in retaining their prosperity while others failed. In most cases, he observed individual habits, characteristics, and behavior as contributory factors in a person's steady progress or downfall. Buddha readily offered guidance to his wealthy lay disciples to enable them to avoid disasters and to stabilize their achievement. He formulated a set of principles that would specifically help his lay followers to retain their prosperity undiminished. This chapter will put together and elaborate on these principles.

Importantly, we may look at Buddha's philosophy about lay life in order to understand his guidance of laypersons toward stability in success. As Buddha observed, short-lived prosperity would not be success at all. He stated that a layperson's aim should be not only to become prosperous but also to maintain prosperity. Striving for material success, one should wish to have unfading affluence throughout life.[2] This philosophy seemingly motivated Buddha to guide his lay community members toward lifelong success.

Let us take for discussion each of Buddha's recommendations that guides a layperson's effort to retain prosperity. We focus mainly on *Vyagghapajja* and *Pattakamma Suttas* in the *Anguttara Nikaya* and *Sigalovada Sutta* in the *Digha Nikaya*.

Step 1: Take actions to protect wealth

Protective actions, according to Buddha's instructions, are one of the most important requirements for a person to safeguard his or her prosperity. "A layperson has obtained wealth through right effort, skill, and just means," Buddha remarked. "He or she should take actions to protect it from the king, thieves, fire, water, and unfriendly relatives."[3]

Buddha's definition of protection reflects the threats that a prosperous person encountered in that society. Close observation reveals that similar threats to undo a wealthy person are also lurking in today's society. Modern law allows the government to confiscate, and financial institutions to take over, personal wealth. Both in conventional and modernized forms, thieves thrive in present society. Fire and flood in our cities constantly cause property damage. After the lapse of over twenty-five centuries, people still experience the same perils that could destroy their wealth.

As Buddha suggested, a wealthy person may guard wealth from governmental interference by acquiring it in the rightful way and by fulfilling his or her duties to the government. Whenever Buddha encouraged people toward prosperity, he reminded them of the just means through which wealth should be acquired. *Dhammikehi dhammaladdhehi* (using rightful means and acquired through harmless means)[4] was the phrase he constantly used to signify the "just effort for material success." Buddha indicated that, by following just means, a successful person would reduce the risk of having the government take over his or her wealth.

Also, the individual and the government, according to Buddha, are bound together by duties and responsibilities. As previously noted, payment of taxes is a primary duty of the individual toward the government. Buddha used the word *rajabali* to mean the portion of wealth that an individual should give to the government.[5] Once these duties are fulfilled, the wealthy person has eliminated the threat of takeover by the government.

During Buddha's time, people protected their wealth from thieves by keeping it in their personal possession, but today people leave their wealth with others—e.g., financial institutions—for maximum protection. In this situation, one can follow Buddha's teaching of protection by choosing the most trustworthy institutions at which to deposit and invest one's money. The fall of large institutions due to corruption and other reasons indicates that we need to invest wealth wisely in order to protect it from modern-day thieves.

Buddha also explained that protection includes taking action to safeguard wealth "from fire and water" (*aggito va udakato va*).[6] Modern versions of this protection are to have fire alarms and extinguishers, to buy fire insurance, and, if necessary, to have flood insurance. These precautionary actions will provide protection to property and wealth were an unexpected tragedy to occur.

Taking steps to safeguard wealth "from unfriendly relatives" (*appiyato dayadato*) is another protective action, from Buddha's viewpoint. This advice may have been more relevant in Buddha's own time, but we can hardly rule out its applicability in today's society. Some people, for example, would give their relatives substantial loans based on mere trust. However, the beneficiary would betray all trust, never returning the loan. In some cultures, parents and grandparents are the most vulnerable to this danger. Adult children and in-laws might squeeze wealth out of their elderly relatives. These occurrences suggest that steps to protect wealth from unfriendly relatives are a genuine need for some people in today's society.

Overall, Buddha strongly encouraged his lay community to take the necessary steps to protect their wealth. That protection is imperative for a person to enjoy lifelong prosperity. The term *arakkha sampada*, which Buddha used to identify the protection of wealth, indicates its overwhelming importance. This phrase means that taking steps to protect wealth is similar to fulfilling a notable accomplishment.

Step 2: Select wise and upright people for companionship and consultation

Buddha consistently reminded his followers that wise and upright people are an asset to the prosperous person in order to shield his or her prosperity. According to Buddha's advice to Dighajanu, a young man who sought Buddha's guidance, relationships with such people would provide "future benefits and happiness" to those who live a secular life, "accepting gold and silver."[7] Again, Buddha told young Sigala that association with undisciplined and morally corrupt people is a "channel through which wealth would disappear."[8] He discussed in detail how relationships would either protect or destroy individual wealth.

A mentor, according to Buddha's wisdom, can be identified by four characteristics: discipline, inner development, mental strength, and wisdom. Buddha explained that a person's use of language, reaction to tragic situations, and ideas expressed in discussions would constantly shed light on his or her qualifications as a mentor. Essentially, one should maintain a long relationship with a person and reflect on his or her behavior thoughtfully in order to decide whether he or she is qualified to be a mentor.[9] Buddha instructed his lay community members to keep in contact with qualified mentors, to converse with them, and especially to discuss ideas with them. By doing so, a layperson may develop his or her own personality and gain knowledge and skills. This experience would further enhance the layperson's prosperity.

In addition, the wise choice of close companions would also play a crucial role in the layperson's effort to consolidate success. Buddha identified the significant role of social forces, environmental factors, and peer influences in a person's life. He gave a vivid description of people whose companionship would lead to the decline of success. For instance, some people would shower the person with extravagant praise, offer too little help, and, in return, anticipate unrealistic advantages.[10] Some others, even though they might be able to fulfill a request made by the friend, would apologize, saying, "Sorry, if you had asked me earlier, I would have done that," or "Not now, perhaps in the future."[11] Some would approve both the wholesome and the unwholesome actions of their friend, and praise him or her in their presence but discredit the friend at other times. They might also entice a successful person into drinking, gambling, and similar harmful habits.[12]

Buddha cautioned that the physical appearance of these companions, or their immediate display of impressive behavior, may not offer enough, or true, evidence to evaluate them. One needs to observe their behavior for a certain period of time and then evaluate it in order to know them correctly. One who wishes for more prosperity should avoid "enemies in the guise of friends."[13]

Elaborating further, Buddha went on to describe some salient characteristics of a genuine friend who would contribute to one's success. These characteristics include providing help in time of need, keeping secrets, retaining unchanged affection, and offering advice to correct a friend's harmful habits, such as drinking. Furthermore, honest friendship between two persons may be detected in their inclination to speak well of each other in the company of other people.[14] Association with friends who display these traits would pave the way for a layperson to strengthen his or her success.

Step 3: Spend according to a financial plan

Buddha recommended a financial plan for the family or the individual in order to safeguard and enhance the success already achieved. He specifically mentioned that the person who prefers a high-class lifestyle despite achieving only a small income would soon diminish his or her wealth. A financial plan should guide the layperson to spend, invest, and save his or her income wisely.

The following words of Buddha both emphasize the importance of a financial plan and provide a clue to what he meant by balanced spending:

> The wise layperson knows the amount of his or her income and expenses, and, with that knowledge, he or she calculates thus: "My income does not exceed my expenses, nor do my expenses make up too meager a portion of my total income." An experienced user of a scale [with two trays of equal weight hanging

> from the ends of the beam] knows, "If I put this or that weight
> on this tray, the other tray will rise or fall to this or that level."
> Similarly, the householder must know how to balance the
> amount of his or her expenses.[15]

This quotation indicates that spending should be proportionate to
income. Only a certain percentage of income should be taken for personal use. As discussed in Chapter Two, Buddha suggested that, for a
businessperson in particular, a quarter of the total income would be
the right portion for personal use. The rest of the wealth is for invest-
ment and saving.

Significantly, these suggested restrictions are not meant to suppress a layperson's enjoyment of life. As discussed in Chapter One,
Buddha maintained that one's wealth should be used for one's own
benefit and happiness. However, one needs to be aware that the percentage allocated for use should be proportionate to the income one
receives. Failure to honor this golden rule would lead an individual to
numerous problems.

Nowhere other than in modern society is this advice so useful for
the public. Persuasion is at work in full force to entice every individual
into an extravagant style of living. Alluring advertisements constantly
pound the images of attractive cars, grand houses, and various enticing products into people's minds. Their appeal has become so powerful
that an elegant style of living through whatever means has almost become the norm in modern society. Many people fall prey to this popular expectation and, in consequence, fail to adopt a sensible financial
plan.

Social pressure, on the other hand, makes some people lose patience
with their balanced spending. Society in general tends to respect people
on the basis of their belongings: their vehicles, houses, and other material items. Brainwashed by these social values, some clearly fail to adopt
a prudent financial plan. Instead, they use so-called easy payment and
monthly installment methods to purchase a plethora of items. Without
a judicious spending plan, they actually make others prosperous by pay-

ing huge amounts of interest while risking their own prosperity. These people will find Buddha's suggestion of a financial plan immensely beneficial.

As Buddha observed, to be free of loan payments is a great relief (*anana sukha*) for the layperson.[16] Dependence on loans to enjoy a lavish lifestyle, according to Buddha, is one of the biggest mistakes a layperson could ever make. He compared such a person to a man who would pluck all the fruits from a tree to eat only what is ripe.[17]

Step 4: Take steps for self-protection

Buddha was also concerned about the dangers to a wealthy layperson's life and to the lives of his or her family members. He specifically stated that one should take precautionary actions to protect oneself and the entire family from potentially dangerous situations. Using the wealth obtained through rightful means, "a wealthy person should take steps for self-defense, and should make life secure."[18]

The underlying concept of these protective measures is that life is worth living happily and peacefully with family members. As previously mentioned, a wealthy person, according to Buddha's philosophy, should have a great expectation: "I must live a long life with my family members and teachers."[19] Precautionary actions would make this objective attainable.

Five factors may pose a threat to the personal safety and security of a wealthy person. They are fire, water, the law, thieves, and unfriendly relatives. As discussed in this chapter, Buddha had already cited the same causes as potential dangers to the wealth of a person. He repeated these factors as possible threats to a prosperous person's life seemingly because he expected personal safety to be a major concern in one's life. Self-protection means taking the necessary steps to prevent the dangers coming from these sources.[20]

According to Buddha, "living at a suitable place" brings many benefits for a layperson.[21] On the one hand, the benefits can be spiritual. On the other hand, they enhance personal safety. We assume that Buddha advised his lay followers to avoid crime-infested neighborhoods, as well as areas prone to flooding. He mentioned villages washed away by flood.[22] He noted that fear, danger, and misfortune all come from immature and opportunistic people (*bala*), not from mature and virtuous people (*pandita*).[23] These remarks shed light on his advice to live in safe areas for protection—areas where natural dangers and human disturbances are minimal.

Protection of oneself and one's family members from punishment by the government is another important aspect of security. The entire family should respect the law of the land, and one's own actions, including how one makes money, should cause no harm to society. As mentioned in this chapter, Buddha reiterated that wealth should be acquired lawfully and that one must show one's dutifulness to the government by paying taxes. Whenever he explained how a layperson should use his or her wealth, Buddha mentioned that a portion should go to the government. These are required steps to protect oneself and one's family members from the law.

With regard to avoiding tragic situations caused by criminals or by accidents, Buddha made a simple but greatly effective suggestion: "Do not travel at a dangerous time."[24] He explained that the person who "consistently walks along streets" risks his or her life and leaves family members in danger.[25]

"Walking along streets at dangerous hours" is an ancient phrase which, in a modern sense, also means "driving and stopping at unsafe places at risky times." In today's world, a large number of crimes, including rapes, robberies, and murders, do occur at night near cash machines and at isolated service stations and convenience stores. Also, danger lurks when adults leave their children at home during an unsafe time, such as at night. Thus, Buddha's advice is perfectly applicable to the present time.

Overall, taking precautionary actions, according to Buddha's reflection, is the key to protecting oneself and one's family members from dangerous situations. These actions would avert the possible dangers to one's own life and those of one's family. Protection of oneself and one's family is also the protection of one's own prosperity.

Step 5: Take the necessary steps at the right time

The most important requirement for any kind of success appears over and over again. Chapter Three has already drawn attention to how essential timing is in the initiation of any successful effort. Buddha identified the same factor as a necessity to maintain prosperity.

As Buddha saw it, timely action strengthens success in two ways. First, by removing disruptions, it steadies the progress already achieved. Next, timing persuades others—coworkers, employees, and associates—to act on time. [26] Advising King Kosala, Buddha said that timely action would protect and increase the king's wealth. In the same discussion, Buddha clarified that, when the king followed the timing principle, others would do the same. This influence also would secure and facilitate the king's progress.

As noted in the previous chapter, taking timely actions means the opposite of laziness, lethargy, negligence, procrastination, or any other word that suggests lack of desire, energy, or readiness to do the necessary actions. To overcome physical and mental inaction means not only to stimulate success but also to steady it.

Step 6: Avoid indulgence in romantic relationships

In an extended simile, Buddha compared a person's wealth to the crystal waters in a beautiful pond. Engagement in multiple sexual relationships is a wide-open canal that would remove the water and make the pond empty. Avoidance of such relationships seals off the canal that drains wealth.[27]

Of course, Buddha never intended to suppress the sex life of an individual, but he advised his lay followers to be moderate if they were to retain their success. *Itthidhutto* (becoming a woman-hunter) is the term Buddha used to suggest indulgence in sexual relationships. This term indicates a sort of addiction to romantic relationships. That addiction, according to Buddha, is a formidable threat to a successful person.

We have only to observe present society to grasp the truth of this statement. With so few restrictions on a person's sex life, people in some societies enjoy considerable freedom to seek many sexual partners. The so-called enjoyment, however, is not a free adventure. Expensive gifts, constant visits to restaurants and entertainment centers, and other expenses might be a burden for a man if he wishes to sustain several sexual relationships. Children from these relationships would make the situation more burdensome. Although fatherhood is a blessing, paying childcare benefits for several children might be difficult, even for an extremely rich person. One's progress may flounder under such heavy financial burdens.

In Buddha's own words, "whatever one earns dwindles away" when one becomes involved in multiple sexual relationships.[28] Avoidance of such connections would contribute to the stability and improvement of one's prosperity.

Step 7: Refrain from addiction to intoxicants

Metaphorically, addiction to intoxicants is another "channel that pours out individual wealth."[29] Analyzing the problem, Buddha noted that the side effects of this dangerous habit would be the cause of ruin. Addiction to intoxication would cause a host of adverse effects: sickness, bad reputation, shamelessness, mental disability, conflicts, and legal problems.[30] These factors would pose a serious threat to one's prosperity.

Our own society provides us with more than enough examples to illustrate this point. Health problems caused by drug abuse, smoking, and alcohol use are major killers today. A kidney or heart problem connected with alcoholism, or lung cancer stemming from smoking, could instantly reverse years of progress in one's life. Also, bitter conflicts may arise in a family when one of the spouses becomes an alcoholic or a drug addict. Divorce and a child custody battle might follow, causing agony and financial loss. As a result, steady family progress would experience a severe blow.

A special note about the connection between drug or alcohol abuse and damaging legal problems seems necessary. Obviously, alcoholism and drug addiction give rise to numerous risky practices, such as drunk driving and drug trafficking. These illegal practices lead to legal battles that could cause irreversible drawbacks. For a person who has just settled down in life, these problems are hardly tolerable.

So, refraining from addiction to intoxicants such as alcohol, tobacco, and drugs clearly removes some causes that would rob a person's success. It also paves the way for a mentally and physically vigorous life. To quote Buddha's own words, non-addiction to intoxicants is an *ayamukha,* which means "a source of more prosperity."[31]

Step 8: Do away with gambling habits

The other habit that Buddha saw as threatening to a person's success is compulsive gambling. This habit, according to Buddha's clarification, would cause many negative consequences such as grief and loss of friendship, confidence, and wealth. He called this dangerous practice "a wide opening that drains wealth."[32]

Buddha always opposed gambling mainly because he promoted human skill rather than individual luck as a means to success. To him, dependence on luck is a denial of human ability to succeed. By choosing the wrong path, an addicted gambler would end up in a wilderness rather than in the fortunate situation he or she dreams of.

The face of gambling has undergone many changes today. Lotteries, casino centers, and online betting dominate organized and legalized forms of gambling. However, what Buddha noticed as negative consequences of compulsive gambling have hardly changed. A habitual gambler even today will always lose wealth, lament over his or her financial failures, and fail to secure the trust and confidence of important people.

Each of these negative effects plays its own role, dragging the person down the ladder of success. Keeping oneself away from this dangerous habit is an act of blocking another "channel of dissipating wealth."[33]

Step 9: Avoid indulgence in entertainment

Finally, Buddha instructed his lay followers to avoid indulgence in entertainment in order to keep their prosperity intact. He noticed that a person who constantly watches "dancing, singing, music, plays, and performances" tends to experience a decline in his or her success.[34]

The key word in this piece of advice is *abhi+charano*. It means "more than usual visits" to festivities where all sorts of merrymaking are going on. Buddha never asked his lay followers to abstain from entertainment. Instead, he instructed them to know the limits of enjoyment. Exceeding the limits would pose a threat to the progress already achieved.

Buddha cited dancing, singing, music, storytelling, and musical performances as addictive types of entertainment for transitory satisfaction. However, in today's world, "entertainment" comes in vastly modified forms. Outside the home, people find theaters, cinemas, playgrounds, nightclubs, and many other places to entertain them. At home, they have an "entertainment center," which provides "couch entertainment" in multiple forms. Besides, they have electronic media in each room for each family member's private enjoyment. All these sources of enjoyment can be included in what Buddha called entertainment.

Addiction to any of them, according to Buddha's point of view, would undermine the progress one has already achieved in life. Even though Buddha allowed his lay followers to find joy in entertainment, he did not want them to exceed the limits and obstruct their progress.

Summary

Overall, Buddha offered invaluable advice and guidance to his lay followers to strengthen their success and to retain it undiminished throughout their lives. He urged them to take steps to protect wealth, to consult and associate with wise people, to take timely actions, to use wealth according to a plan, and to be concerned about self-protection. Buddha also requested them to avoid indulgence in romantic relationships, intoxicants, gambling, and entertainment. These guidelines suggest that professionalism, farsightedness, and behavior adjustment are the key factors for lifelong prosperity. Even today, one can follow these instructions to achieve the intended results.

Chapter Five

Four Steps to Select People for Closer Relationships

Neither their appearance nor a brief positive impression depicts a true picture of people.

Buddha, the *Kindred Sayings*

"Careful selection of people for close relationships" was an overwhelmingly important topic in Buddha's teaching. He once advised his disciples to choose a solitary life, similar to that of a lonely rhinoceros, if they failed to find suitable associates.[1] This remark foretells Buddha's emphasis on the right choice of people for close association. Such a selection is important because it could contribute to peaceful and lasting relationships. Buddha indicated that we may choose compatible people by following a process that consists of several steps. We find these steps widely discussed throughout the *Sutta Pitaka*. Let us put them together to gain a comprehensive understanding of how to find close companions and associates.

Buddha's instructions on how to select people for personal relationships do not mean that we should reject some people as unsuitable. Buddha never asked his disciples to condemn an incompatible, or even an unpleasant and troublesome, person. Instead, he advised them to understand his or her nature, show compassion, and provide an opportunity for improvement. Yet, compatibility is a dependable criterion to select individuals for close relationships, and Buddha's instructions were meant to facilitate this effort.

The *Sutta Pitaka* offered the following steps that Buddha recommended in order for his disciples to find the most compatible partners and associates:

Step 1: Leave aside unproven traditional criteria

Traditional beliefs during Buddha's time claimed that race and caste should be the main criteria for selecting people for close ties, including marriage. Members of the Shudra caste, for instance, could maintain close links only with other Shudras. In marriage, in particular, they had to select only the people of their own caste. Buddha

launched a tireless and fruitful campaign against these irrational beliefs. He once mentioned that one should not even ask a person about
his or her caste or race as a criterion to reject or accept that person.[2]
He encouraged his followers to leave aside a person's race, caste, gender, and external appearance in order to accept him or her for a close
relationship.

This clarification seems important not only to find people for
companionship but also to select individuals for marriage. In other
words, caste, race, or other social differences should not be a barrier when people select their intimate partners. While discussing
the elements of a successful marriage, Buddha never advised his lay
disciples to select partners only from their own caste, race, or creed.
Rather, compatibility in attitudes and behavior was one of the factors
that he constantly emphasized for a successful marital relationship.

Buddha stressed throughout his speeches the danger of forming
intimate relationships with *bala*, a technical term for an inadequately
developed and incompatible person.[3] A *pandita*, or a well-developed
and compatible person, whom Buddha recommended for a close relationship, can be selected from any caste, race, or social group irrespective of all differences. Buddha's statement that not birth but upright
conduct and inner development determine a person's importance[4]
confirms this criterion.

Similarly, gender, according to Buddha's teaching, is no barrier to
men and women to maintain any close association for a common goal.
For instance, Buddha's ordained male and female disciples maintained
close relationships in their efforts to achieve self-purification and to
take Buddha's teaching to society. Buddha especially mentioned that
female disciples should live close to male disciples for safety and counseling, and that male disciples should regularly visit and communicate
with their female counterparts.[5] This association was based on the
understanding of each person's objectives rather than on mutual attachment. Both sexes were advised to be mindful about their passion
and to keep it in check. Male disciples called the females "sisters," and

both sexes kept in close contact with each other, successfully continuing their mission.

So, the first step in selecting suitable people for association and intimate relationships is to disregard caste, class, race, creed, and similar attributes as a criterion. From Buddha's point of view, these factors have no reason to justify their consideration.

Step 2: Be cautious about first impression and initial understanding of people

While Buddha thus rejected traditional attitudes as criteria for selecting associates, he also discouraged people's reliance on their first impression and initial feelings about others. For example, some individuals may demonstrate great skill in presenting themselves as perfectly suitable for successful relationships. However, we should refrain from leaping to the conclusion that their self-portrayal is a genuine reflection of their true nature.

The following two stanzas uttered by Buddha summarize this point:

> People cannot be known well by their appearance,
> Nor can they be trusted after a brief impression.
> Yes, the undisciplined may roam in the world
> In the attire of the well-disciplined.
>
> Some adorn their unpleasantness
> With pretended suave action
> Like a clay earring or brass
> Painted with glittering gold.[6]

These poems suggest the danger of leaping to conclusions about people. On the one hand, the appearance of some people is not a dependable criterion for us to form a genuine picture of them. The word Buddha used in this utterance to suggest appearance is *vannarupa*. It means both "physical outlook" and "behavior." Both professional appearance and cultured behavior are included in this term as being insufficient evidence to evaluate a person.

On the other hand, a brief association would also fail to provide a clear understanding about people. Buddha used *ittaradassana* to suggest a short association. Literally, it means "seeing little." For a short period of time, people may successfully conceal their true nature. Therefore, a brief association would not reflect their actual behavior and thinking.

Notably, however, this advice does not mean that those who are pleasant and courteous at the beginning of a relationship should be doubted. Inherently pleasant people, according to our own experience, may immediately present themselves as such. The important point is that insincere people also may pose as nice people. Therefore, Buddha taught that we should not depend on first impression or short-term experience to accept people as compatible.

Step 3: Follow the process of association, observation, and evaluation

Having rejected the insufficient criteria discussed above, Buddha offered his followers a process to acquire a better understanding of people. This understanding would enable them to select compatible people for closer relationships. Such a selection would, in turn, contribute to the construction of healthier and stronger relationships. This process is as follows:

1. Associate with a person for a certain period of time.
2. Observe and evaluate his or her words and actions.[7]

Buddha explained these steps to King Kosala when the king, perhaps jokingly, introduced to Buddha a group of his secret agents posing as ascetics. First, King Kosala respectfully greeted the spies in front of Buddha. After they left, the king told Buddha, "Those ascetics have selected the path for spiritual progress." Buddha replied that the king's judgment would be wrong because he (the king) did not possess enough evidence to support his claim.

"With a close relationship, you can [begin to] understand others' discipline, purity, and wisdom," explained Buddha. "Still, the relationship should extend over a certain period of time, not a short duration."[8] He emphatically stated that a short-term relationship would be insufficient to gain a better knowledge about others. People unfold themselves as time goes by. We need to associate with them and observe their behavior closely in order to understand their true nature.

After observation, we may think over and compare and contrast the behavior already observed. Buddha used the word *manasikaroti* to signify this process. This word conveys several meanings, such as "ponder," "bear in mind," and "think over." Altogether, it denotes "evaluation of behavior."

Wisdom, according to Buddha, is an important requirement to make this evaluation accurate. The Pali word used in this context is *pannavata*, which means "by the person who uses knowledge, skill, and wisdom." Evaluation should have a rational basis. We may compare, contrast, and interpret various forms of behavior we have already observed. Buddha mentioned on several occasions that behavior would constantly reflect one's character. A rational evaluation would allow us to obtain a clear picture of the person whom we have known for a certain period of time.

The importance of this evaluation lies in the conclusion that we need to find people with well-developed personalities with whom to establish close relationships. The previous chapter referred to Buddha's statement that all fears and worries come from inadequately developed people, not from people with wisdom.[9] Correct evaluation of behavior would allow us to find wise people who would cause no fear or worries.

Step 4: Consider compatibility

The objective of the entire process of association, observation, and evaluation is to decide the person's suitability for a committed relationship. Compatibility is the main issue at this point. Buddha stated that closely connected people should be compatible in order for them to maintain healthy relationships.

What is compatibility?

As already discussed in this chapter, the word "compatibility," according to Buddha's definition, does not mean the two persons' belonging to the same caste, social class, or race. He rejected these social truths as fragile and baseless. From Buddha's point of view, compatibility means the matching behavior and attitudes of the two persons. Finding out this similarity is the objective of the entire process of association, observation, and evaluation.

Buddha especially elaborated on the importance of matching attitudes and behavior for a successful marital relationship. He said that both partners can be pleasant to each other when they have the following four similarities:

Similar belief in spiritual development

Similar respect for self-discipline

Similar respect for humanistic practices

Similar level of wisdom[10]

These similarities are so important for a peaceful marital relationship that close attention to each of them seems necessary.

A. Similar belief in spiritual development

Buddha said, "Both partners should have similar beliefs about spiritual development" (*ubho janapatiyo samasaddha*) in order for them to establish and maintain a healthy relationship. This statement does not necessarily mean that both of them should follow a spiritual path rigorously. Rather, it means that, if one partner maintains strong respect for spiritual beliefs and practices while the other shows total disregard for them, the two are simply incompatible.

Their different views about rebirth, creation, development of extraperceptive powers, divinity, and prayer may be cited as examples. Both being nonbelievers in after-death existence, for instance, would be better than one being a believer in, and the other a doubter of, rebirth or resurrection. Compatibility in spiritual beliefs and practices means that both partners have matching views and practices in spiritual matters.

B. Similar respect for self-discipline

The next type of compatibility of two people, according to Buddha's observation, is both partners' similar regard for self-discipline (*samasila*). When one is well-disciplined and the other unscrupulous, the two persons' incompatibility becomes obvious. This difference will cause problems in the relationship.

Chapter Twelve will present a thorough discussion of what Buddha meant by "self-discipline" for the layperson. In brief, one's respect for such moral practices as abstinence from destroying life and stealing are examples of self-discipline. Buddha suggested that, if one is concerned about and skillful in self-discipline, so also should one's marital partner be. Such compatibility would make the relationship smooth and pleasant.

C. Similar respect for humanistic practices

Buddha recognized both partners' similar respect for humanity as another sign of compatibility. Some people may be naturally self-centered while others are altruistic. A marriage where each spouse belongs to one of the two different groups may be a mismatch because of their incompatible attitudes and behavior.

As Buddha specified, humanistic practices mean *dana* (also known as *caga*), or the layperson's voluntary contribution to society. *Dana* is threefold: giving money and material objects, helping to protect life, and teaching and giving moral support, instructions, and guidance. One spouse's readiness and the other's reluctance to practice *dana* suggest clear incompatibility of the two persons.

D. Similar level of wisdom

Various speeches of Buddha suggest that the term "wisdom" conveys a broad meaning, which includes knowledge, skill, intellectual strength, emotional maturity, attitudinal improvement, and reasoning power. Buddha remarked that the two partners' similarities in these areas (*samapanna*) would denote their compatibility.

Again, this suggestion does not mean that both of them should have the same education, intellectual abilities, and so forth. Instead, it means that a wide difference in these areas would cause incompatibility, which might lead to conflicts in the relationship. Buddha implied that his lay disciples should be aware of this factor when they select partners for marriage.

Summary

Buddha provided useful instructions to his lay community for selecting people for companionship and intimate relationships. His assertion is that traditional, stereotypical attitudes about people would offer no clue to accepting or rejecting people for close ties. Similarly, intuition and first impression are unreliable criteria to judge the compatibility of people. Buddha suggested, instead, that association with people and observation and evaluation of their behavior would allow us to decide on their suitability for close association. Selecting people for marriage, in particular, should be based on mutual compatibility. A similar concern for spiritual development, self-discipline, and humanistic practices, along with a similar level of wisdom, defines the compatibility of two partners.

Chapter Six

Tips to Establish a Great Marital Partnership

When both partners trust each other, use pleasant words to communicate with each other, have self-discipline, and maintain upright conduct, their progress increases, and pleasant life is born!

Buddha, the *Gradual Sayings*

As discussed in the previous chapter, careful selection of companions, according to Buddha, is merely a prerequisite for healthy relationships: it only brings together two compatible, mutually acceptable individuals. Buddha's wisdom shows us that, for a marital relationship to run smoothly, several more necessities should be met. Essentially, the attitudes and behavior of both partners should reach the standard of mutual satisfaction. The present chapter will discuss this crucial requirement in detail, simultaneously highlighting its applicability to present-day life.

From Buddha's standpoint, the relationship between a man and a woman can be raised to the level of "a union between a god and a goddess."[1] This metaphor suggests the potential peacefulness and happiness inherent in such a relationship. Buddha maintained that, with developed attitudes and behavior habits, both partners would be able to make their relationship blissful for each other.

My rights or my duty and obligation?

Fulfillment of duties and obligations, as observed by Buddha, is more persuasive for each partner in a marriage than fighting for rights. Thus, he recommended dutifulness and obligation as powerful concepts to establish a successful marital relationship.[2] The philosophy goes as follows: when both persons are mindful about their duties and obligations, neither may tend to misuse the other. In this situation, a need to fight for rights would rarely arise. Importantly, Buddha did not identify this approach as a magic solution to all conflicts between two mates. Rather, he held that fulfillment of duties and obligations is an important step to maintain a blissful relationship between two partners.

What are, actually, the meanings of "dutifulness" and "obligation" as Buddha identified them? He used several words such as *upakara* and *paccupatthana* to mean "dutifulness" and *paccupakara* and *anu-kampa* to denote "obligation." His definitions of these words have not been preserved, but his description of the actions related to the words presents a clear view of what he meant by them.

Dutifulness is the natural and selfless commitment associated with each person's position in a relationship. As explained in *Sigalovada Sutta*, parents' provision of help, care, food, and guidance to children can be taken as a clear example of duty. One's dutifulness in a relationship is not conditional on the gratefulness of the other person in that relationship but is intrinsic to one's own position in the relationship.

Obligation, as it was explained in the same Sutta, means one's gratefulness to, or responsibility for, the other person who has already fulfilled his or her own duty. For instance, "showing kindness to her husband" is an obligation of a wife because her husband has already shown respect to her through his words and deeds. The sentence "Because they supported me, I will support them" clarifies the concept of obligation. While duty is inherent in one's position in a relationship, obligation is conditional to the other person's dutifulness in the same relationship.

Buddha believed that both duty and obligation in a relationship would strengthen the connection between two persons by making both individuals beneficial to each other. Balanced usefulness of one person to the other is the theme behind dutifulness and obligation. We notice that some marital partners fail to accomplish their duty and obligation toward the other but still insist on the other person's observation of the same. This approach may very well be called misuse or abuse. Such a situation would certainly give rise to conflicts in a marital relationship.

Specific duties and obligations in a male-female partnership

Having stressed the importance of dutifulness and obligation in a successful union between a man and a woman, Buddha also recommended specific duties and obligatory acts for both partners.[3] While some of these recommendations reflect the values in Buddha's society, we find timeless practicability and effectiveness behind their social and historical outlook. Let us briefly focus on the five kinds of duties and obligations Buddha recommended for each partner. First, he suggested that the male partner needs to observe the following:

1. Show respect to her

Buddha lived in an era in which men hardly paid attention to women's rights and dignity. At a time when a wife was expected to please her husband and raise children, Buddha made the revolutionary assertion that a man should show respect to his wife in order to make the relationship happy and peaceful. The Pali word he used to suggest this respect is *sammananaya*, which means "with respect and admiration."

Importantly, this duty is the very first of the five duties Buddha requested a husband to fulfill. Buddha brought it to the forefront seemingly because of its overwhelming importance for a healthy marital relationship. All other duties assigned to the male partner in a relationship seem secondary to respect. Whatever he does for his female partner would be shallow and worthless if the husband fails to do it with genuine respect for her.

Different speeches of Buddha provide more details about the respect that is crucial in a healthy interpersonal relationship. Importantly, respect should not be just a superficial verbal expression. Instead, respect needs to originate from within and become visible through words and deeds. In a broader sense, loving-kindness symbolizes respect. The feeling of genuine love and compassion should precede verbal and physical expressions of love. From Buddha's standpoint, the female partner in a union deserves that respect from her male partner. She is not the personal property of her husband, who would manipulate her at will. Instead, she is an equal, respectable partner in the relationship.

2. Refrain from using words that might hurt her

This habit is connected to the first one since refraining from using hurtful words is also a way of showing respect. Still, to ensure the consistency of a male partner's respectful behavior toward his beloved, Buddha asked him to follow this principle closely. Instead of showering her with sweet words when necessary and scolding her at other times, a husband must always be mindful of his words. He should not only use pleasant words but also refrain from using harsh words whenever he communicates with her and talks to others about her. Buddha's phrase *avamananaya* indicates this requirement.

Throughout his public speeches, Buddha maintained that harshness would never solve problems or bring people closer. This theory seems particularly valid in a marital relationship. Unpleasant words would cause the wife to resist and to devalue her husband's personality. Buddha has clearly touched upon the soft nature of women and reminded husbands not to take advantage of it. Instead of trying to intimidate her with harsh behavior, a husband should adhere to a gentle pattern of communication. This approach will contribute to a pleasant relationship between the two.

3. Practice faithfulness

A husband must first be mindful about his own faithfulness to his wife before he begins to inquire about her faithfulness to him. The word *anaticariyaya* indicates this important need. Buddha consistently reminded married men not to seduce women. He used various techniques, including self-reflection and understanding, to discourage men from having extramarital relationships:

> If a certain person seduces my wife, I would not tolerate that person. Similarly, if I seduce somebody else's wife, he will not like me, either. With this awareness, I must refrain from seducing women.[4]

A husband's introspection, understanding, and rational and ethical resolution would thus enable him to remain faithful to his wife. While admitting impulsive sex urge as the most powerful and predominant human desire,[5] Buddha instructed men to handle it responsibly for the sake of their family life.

4. Give up dominance

Buddha persuaded men to give up dominance if they wished to maintain a blissful relationship with their female partners. Buddha's Pali phrase *issariya vossagga* used in this context tells it all. *Issariya* means "authority" or "power." *Vossagga* conveys the meaning of "relaxation," or "relinquishment." Taken together, the two words mean a man's "giving up of dominating behavior" in a marital relationship.

With this recommendation, Buddha suggested a greatly effective means for men to strengthen their relationships with women. Some men would still believe that they are the superior authority in a marriage. "I am the person who makes decisions, and my wife must agree with me," a husband would assert. Buddha claimed that men need to depart from this mentality for the sake of a successful relationship.

A man's giving up of authority, on the other hand, does not mean allowing the female partner to make all decisions. Rather, Buddha encouraged both of them to make decisions together and follow the decisions harmoniously instead of allowing one to dominate the other. A wife, according to Buddha, should never be her husband's puppet; neither should he be hers. On a different occasion, Buddha explained that a successful wife can be mother-like, sister-like, or friend-like.[6] This remark supports the view that Buddha asked both partners in a marital relationship to share the authority. That sharing would allow both of them to coexist peacefully.

5. Respect her fondness for beauty

Buddha identified women as admirers of beauty. He encouraged men to show respect for their female partners' penchant for beautiful objects. Buddha insinuated that this approach, if men took it, would make their female partners happy, and bring two marital partners closer to each other.

The phrase *alankara anuppadana* indicates men's respect for their female partners' desire for beautiful objects. *Alankara* stands for anything attractive, such as pretty clothes and ornaments. *Anuppadana* means "giving as a present." Buddha remarked that men should provide their beloved partners with beautiful objects.

Buddha's expression of this duty reflects the best way a man in that society could show his respect for his female partner's love of beauty. During Buddha's time, women did not go shopping and select what they wanted to buy. Usually men visited marketplaces, where they would buy the requirements for the entire household. In that social setting, women usually requested their male partners to bring home what they (women) wanted. A man's "giving of beautiful items" to his female partner suggests his respect for that request. Because he uses family resources to purchase necessary items for the household, he should also buy what his female partner would like to have.

What is important for today's relationships is the concept behind a male partner's giving of beautiful items to his beloved. He needs to understand that she is an admirer of beauty. While he would not mind driving a decade-old, rusty truck, she would prefer a beautiful new car or a compact SUV. He would be satisfied with grass in the front yard, but she would prefer flowers and ornamental plants in the garden. A male's respect for his female partner's appreciation of beauty is the rationale behind his providing attractive things for her.

"These are the five treatments a husband should offer to his wife,"[7] Buddha remarked after explaining the duties discussed above. Expecting to establish a mutually rewarding relationship, a man needs to be mindful about these five duties toward his partner. Buddha further noted that, thus treated, she would "feel compassion" toward him.[8] That feeling is the knot that connects her to him and keeps her love untarnished.

What she should do for him

To match the husband's attitudes and behavior as described above, the wife also needs to follow a course of action of her own duties and obligations toward her partner. A wife's successful association with her husband is also based on the concept of give-and-take rather than on forceful insistence on rights. A wife is obliged to fulfill a set of actions for her husband, who completes his own duties and responsibilities.

1. Work in an organized way

A wife's organized approach to her own work, as seen by Buddha, is a useful attribute to maintain an excellent relationship with her husband. The Pali term Buddha used in this context is *susanvihita kammanta hoti.* This phrase does not clarify what kind of work she would do but simply means "[She] should have well-organized work." Apparently, Buddha encouraged a woman to be organized in whatever she did.

Obviously, cooking, housekeeping, and taking care of children, as well as supervising these activities, were an essential part of a woman's work during Buddha's time. In a society in which husbands toiled on farms and at other places, and wives mostly stayed at home, this duty of a wife is understandable.

However, Buddha never confined a female to the chores at home. He was an unequivocal advocate for women's rights and freedom. He admitted that a woman's intellectual strength is equal to that of a man.[9] Based on this fact, we may include in the Pali word *kammanta* any kind of work that suits her skill and interest.

In other words, Buddha's concern was not what kind of work a wife did, but how she did it. While most female followers of Buddha were housewives, some of them were landowners and home-business partners. Whatever their occupations, Buddha encouraged women to do their work in an organized way. He maintained that a woman's self-organization would contribute to a peaceful relationship with her male partner.

2. Handle family relationships

This duty of a wife basically reflects Buddha's society. As previously discussed, most people who sought Buddha's guidance in secular matters were business people and property owners. They would hardly have spent their daytime hours at home. Their wives, meanwhile, had ample time to communicate with relatives and friends, and to deal with household employees and other important people related to work or business. Considering this situation, Buddha seems to have assigned this duty to the female.

Today's world, however, has changed so drastically that we find it difficult to assign the same duty specifically to a wife. With both husband and wife working, or a husband staying at home while his wife works, maintaining relationships with important people is a task that needs to be shared today. Nevertheless, for many families the wife seems to be the most qualified person to handle relationships with others.

This conclusion is based on a woman's natural inclination and knack for such relationships. While most men would prefer to be introverted, women would choose to be otherwise. Women's interests and skills in relationships place them ahead of men to handle family relationships with a host of people. Thus, Buddha's remark that a wife should monitor family relationships with outside people seems relevant for today as well.

3. Be faithful to him

Buddha also emphasized that, similar to a husband's faithful behavior, so also should his wife be faithful to him. This principle emphasizes her abstinence from extramarital relationships; heeding it would further enhance the relationship between a man and a woman.

As mentioned before, Buddha never allowed men to use women as their personal property. A husband has no extra privilege to have more than one sexual relationship while forcing his wife to have only him. Abstinence from sexual misbehavior applies equally to both husband and wife.

As long as a husband remains faithful to his wife and fulfills his duties toward her, she has an obligation to be faithful to him. Chapter Twelve will discuss the point that, when he no longer carries out his own duties and responsibilities, she should have the right to make her own decision.

4. Take steps to protect family wealth

Buddha portrayed men as susceptible to harmful social forces. As indicated in several Suttas, men might become victims of money-wasting habits such as alcoholism, gambling, and unsuitable relationships. In this situation, a wife would be the most suitable person to protect family wealth. Her actions in this regard would strengthen her relationship with her husband.

Buddha also defined what he meant by "protection of wealth." "She should not swindle, save greedily, or waste away the wealth, but protect it," he explained.[10] So, one way for a wife to protect wealth is to regard it as family wealth rather than to use it or keep it as her own personal wealth. Next, she should know how to use it moderately. Mere hoarding or squandering are both extremes.

These steps seem to improve the relationship in two ways. First, her honesty with family wealth would increase his trust in her. Second, her judicious spending would win his respect. Both reactions would contribute to the enhancement of unity and togetherness in the relationship.

5. Show skill and energy

"Skillfulness and energetic engagement in everything she does" is
the next duty that a wife needs to fulfill in order to maintain a successful relationship with her husband.[12] Buddha did not explain, or
rather, the Suttas did not preserve, what "everything" (*sabba kicca*)
would mean, but, undoubtedly, it was not servile duties at home.

As already discussed, Buddha regarded a woman as an equal partner in a relationship with a man. According to her skills and interests,
she was expected to perform an active and responsible role in the family. Organizing a family business, maintaining relationships with others, protecting family wealth, and sharing the duties of raising children are some of the acts that would require her skill and energy.

Her energetic and skillful fulfillment of these duties enhances her
relationship with her partner because it allows her to feel that she is
an active participant in family success. When both partners work toward a common goal, they tend to please each other.

6. Play an active role as his companion and guide

In addition to the five duties that appeared in *Sigalovada Sutta* and
were discussed above, Buddha advised that the woman who plays an
active role as her husband's companion and guide can also become
a successful wife. As he noted, some successful wives, of course, may
regard themselves as followers, but this attitude is not essential for a
happy marriage. A wife needs to be the provider of love, guidance, and
companionship.[13]

Explaining further, Buddha mentioned that some wives would love
and care about their husbands just as a mother attends to a child.
Some would show the right path to their husbands just as an elder sis-
ter does to a younger brother. Others would regard their husbands as
mutual friends and equal partners. As Buddha noticed, these attitudes

and behavior of a wife would contribute immensely to the success of a marital relationship.[14]

Buddha's remarks suggest that a wife should share the responsibilities of the family equally with her husband. Buddha recommended, of course, that a wife should refrain from acts that demean her husband. Nevertheless, he never said that only submissive women would become successful wives. Instead, those who play an active role as mentors, guides, and equal partners with their husbands can contribute to the success of a marriage.

Summary

Buddha offered useful tips for husbands and wives to establish healthy relationships in which both mates would enjoy love, respect, and dignity. Overall, he called attention to fulfillment of individual duties and obligations, rather than to insistence on individual rights, as an important element for the maintenance of healthy personal relationships. Their moral duties, such as faithfulness to each other, would provide an immense psychological satisfaction for both partners. Besides, a balanced distribution of power and a balanced sharing of activities and responsibilities between the two would certainly make each of them feel important in the relationship. These feelings, in turn, would make both partners pleasing to each other.

Chapter Seven

To Be a Proud Parent

"Creator" is a synonym for a parent. "First mentor" and "the beloved" are the other synonyms for a parent. These synonyms are relevant because parents bring children into the world, provide them with manifold help, feed and care for them, and teach them the right path.

Buddha, the *Gradual Sayings*

People often asked Buddha questions about parenthood. They wanted to know the most effective ways of raising children, the duties of being parents, and the techniques for maintaining healthy relationships with their children. "Sir, we are laypersons who live with children," some of them said. "Will you explain to us the right teaching that is beneficial to us?"[1] Others complained about their children's misbehavior and lack of respect, imploring Buddha's help to correct the children and restore the relationships.[2] Buddha listened to these requests and complaints attentively and volunteered to offer his guidance. This chapter will discuss Buddha's tips that would enable mothers and fathers to become special parents.

Providing children with love and physical care

Parental love and care, according to Buddha, is a basic requirement for successful parenthood. By providing nourishment and protection to a child, a father and mother do not make themselves exemplary parents but only take a step on the right path toward becoming so.

In other words, Buddha recognized parents' care and nourishment of their children as an inherent practice of honorable humans. He explained that proper use of a layperson's wealth should include allocation of money for the happiness and comfort of any children that person may have. One who refuses to use one's own wealth for the care of one's children is a "wicked person" (*asappurisa*).[3] These remarks suggest that feeding and taking care of children is a minimum requirement for all parents, rather than a valid reason to consider themselves excellent parents. In his advice to Sigala, Buddha did not even mention such activities as being a part of parental duty. He seems to have suggested that being a parent means one must provide one's children with all kinds of physical care and attention. Becoming a better parent means thinking beyond the children's physical comfort and protection.

In *Mangala Sutta* Buddha cited "caring for children" (*putta san-gaha*) as a "blissful sign" for lay life.[4] Related speeches indicate that what he meant by "caring for" is more than concern for the physical well-being of children. For Buddha, raising a child meant making a baby a great human being. Parents need to make it a goal to help their children achieve inner development, knowledge and skill, and success in life. Parents' triumph in this effort means the realization of their fullest potential in parenthood.

While elaborating on the relationship between parents and children, Buddha assigned in *Sigalovada Sutta* five duties to parents.[5] Fulfillment of these duties would provide a tremendous opportunity for parents not only to establish healthy relationships with their children but also to feel proud about themselves. Let us have a look at each of these duties.

1. Help children refrain from unwholesome conduct

Parents, according to Buddha's definition, are "the first teachers" of their children. He used the term *papa nivarenti* to mean the parental duty of keeping children away from unwholesome conduct. *Papa* means any wrong action done through words, deeds, and thoughts. *Nivarenti* suggests the effort to avoid such actions. Helping their children to refrain from unwholesome acts is a part of parental teaching. Parents should take steps to block the causes that would drag the children into unwholesome acts.

How can parents fulfill this duty successfully? Buddha never believed that a forceful approach, such as physical punishment, would help toward this end. "Everybody is threatened by punishment," Buddha once said, discouraging any form of punishment to anybody.[6] We do not find in the *Sutta Pitaka* a single instance of Buddha's supporting punishment as an effective way to mold children's behavior. Contrary to some people's belief in "spoiling the child by sparing the rod," compassionate Buddha never asked parents to punish their children. His speeches show better ways of helping children to shape their behavior.

Similarly, Buddha never recommended verbal abuse as an effective way to help children to eliminate unwholesome conduct. Speaking generally about harsh language, Buddha noted that the listener's angry reaction would be the result of one's using such language.[7] He went on to say in the same verse that the use of harsh words would only cause frustration and agony for the speaker. Thus, from Buddha's point of view, verbal abuse, like physical punishment, would prevent parents from influencing their children to depart from wrongful conduct.

Advising would be an effective way to prevent children from adopting harmful practices, but parents first need to hold themselves as an example. "One needs to place oneself at the suitable place before one instructs others. Such an adviser does not fall from grace," Buddha commented.[8] This remark shows that, to be a successful adviser, one needs to follow one's own advice. Parents would succeed in persuading their children to abstain from harmful actions when they themselves have abstained from similar actions.

Keeping children away from close companionship with corrupt and immoral friends, according to Buddha, is another step in preventing them from getting used to unwholesome behavior. Sigala was a young boy who had just lost his father and was in a confused state of mind. He did not know how to accept the challenge ahead. Buddha's advice to Sigala symbolizes how he would have asked any parents to guide their children.[9] In particular, Buddha told young Sigala not to maintain close links with morally corrupt people because such relationships would ruin the young man's future. In the same way, Buddha would ask any parent to discourage his or her children from having close connections with immoral people in order to prevent the children from getting accustomed to similar habits.

Overall, taking steps to prevent children from becoming corrupt and immoral is a primary duty of parents, according to Buddha's advice. Instead of leaving it to teachers and priests, parents themselves should show concern and take responsibility for the prevention of their children's acclimatization to personally and socially harmful habits.

2. Lead children to wholesome conduct

While taking steps to prevent children from getting used to unwholesome actions, parents should also promote their children's acquisition of wholesome actions. The Pali term Buddha used in this context is *kalyane nivesenti. Kalyane* means "actions that are beautiful, charming, and virtuous." *Nivesenti* means "establish in" or "be the cause of." Parental duties include the guidance of children toward wholesome conduct.

"Wholesome conduct" represents words, deeds, and thoughts that are motivated by generosity, compassion, and wisdom. In other words, practice of charity (*dana*), improvement of self-discipline (*sila*), and development of the mind (*bhavana*) are the components of wholesome conduct. Buddha encouraged parents to implant these thoughts and actions in their children.

Dedicated commitment from parents would help them achieve this objective. First, as already mentioned, parents need to follow a righteous way of living in order for their children to select a similar path. Next, parents should be aware of who their children's close companions are. Buddha repeatedly stressed that association with *pandita* (virtuous and wise people) would enrich our own characters. Therefore, parents need to persuade their children to keep company with such friends. As Buddha constantly emphasized, skillful communication is an effective technique for responsible people to instill wholesome behavior in others. The same emphasis is applicable to parents who strive to lead their children to wholesome actions.

Still, Buddha's view is that we cannot always bring immediate happiness to another while trying to lead that person toward wholesome actions. Parents, in particular, would find it difficult to please their children with the right advice. Children like to do what brings them immediate satisfaction rather than long-term benefits. They may feel annoyed to hear that what their parents want them to do is the opposite of what they wish to do.

On these occasions, Buddha would ask parents to stand by their values assertively rather than give in. For instance, a child's reluctance to attend a useful workshop at Sunday school should not cause parents to express dislike or frustration. Instead, the parents should insist that, despite the child's objection, he or she should definitely attend it. When parents are convinced that they have taken the right steps for the child's personality development, they must follow these steps without hesitation. These assertive actions may upset the child at the time, but in the long run, they will bring about wholesome effects.

Prince Abhaya, who visited Buddha with a baby in his arms, asked whether Buddha would use harsh words to influence someone's behavior.[10] In response, Buddha said that he would use only pleasant words at the right time. However, he also indicated that, when he knew a certain step to be right, he would never hesitate to take it. "Suppose something got stuck in this baby's throat," Buddha continued. "What would you do?" Abhaya replied that he would somehow take it out. "What about the bleeding and the pain?" Buddha asked. Abhaya said in reply that he would not care because his immediate concern would be to save the child's life. Buddha clarified that certain actions are necessary to lead someone in the right direction even though such actions would not please the person immediately. This example shows that, in their effort to lead children toward wholesome conduct, parents may use emphatic words rather than harsh language and take some steps despite their children's reluctance to follow those steps.

Buddha's own life provides one of the best examples of how a father should commit himself to implanting wholesomeness in a child's mind. His son Rahula was just seven years old when Buddha promised the child "a father's best gift." Having made Rahula a member of the Sangha, Buddha took great care to assist in his personality development. The *Sutta Pitaka* has preserved several of Buddha's speeches addressed to his son. These speeches show Buddha's great concern about Rahula's acquisition of wholesome qualities.

Instead of giving orders, Buddha often appealed to Rahula's rational thinking while assisting his son's personality development. "What is the purpose of a mirror, Rahula?" Buddha once asked his little son. "To see one's own reflection," Rahula replied. "Similarly, one's mind is to reflect on actions," Buddha continued. "You need to evaluate any of your actions in terms of its consequences. If it brings about unwholesome effects for yourself and others, you should prevent yourself from doing it. If it causes wholesome effects, you may do it."[11] This example symbolizes the effective steps a father may choose to instill upright conduct in a child's mind. Buddha's guidance was so perfect that Rahula earned the title "one who is most willing to be trained."

Both by word and deed, Buddha conveyed the message that parents should direct their children toward upright conduct. As a part of their duty, parents should encourage their children to speak wholesome words, to do wholesome deeds, and to develop wholesome thoughts. This guidance should be a main objective of the parents' role, not merely a peripheral matter.

3. Educate children for a profession

The next parental duty, according to *Sigalovada Sutta,* is to provide children with the proper education for a profession. Buddha termed this need *sippam sikkhapeti. Sippa* means "knowledge and skill necessary for a profession." *Sikkhapeti* stands for "teach and educate." Parents may directly help their children's education and also seek the help of qualified people for the same purpose.

This duty signifies that parents should essentially take steps to improve their children's quality of life besides helping the children's personality development. In *Mangala Sutta*, Buddha said, "Vast knowledge, skill, discipline, and pleasant words are great blessings" to a person.[12] "Discipline" and "pleasant words" suggest character development. "Vast knowledge" and "skill" indicate professional qualifications. Parents need to help their children in both areas.

Parents during Buddha's time had very few choices when preparing their children for a profession. Some parents provided the children with their own knowledge. Others left their children with qualified people. Well-to-do families sent their children to such places as Taxila, the capital of Gandhara and the location of the world's first known academic institution. In today's society, however, people have a wide range of opportunities to help their children's education. Sending their children to schools and colleges, and monitoring and spending money on their education are some of the means available to parents to prepare their children for a profession.

The three parental duties discussed so far suggest that the aim of parents is to guide a child toward becoming a complete person. Character adjustment, knowledge, and skill development indicate completeness. To be more specific, a child's departure from unwholesome conduct and his or her acquisition of noble qualities improve the child's inner development. His or her advancement in knowledge and skill makes the child a professionally capable person. Buddha urged parents to make a committed effort to lead a child toward this end.

4. Help children select suitable partners for marriage

Buddha lived in an era during which parental involvement in finding partners for their children seemed most appropriate. On the one hand, without an organized educational system for everyone, the young generation failed to select their partners wisely. On the other hand, without established marital law, married partners left each other without taking any responsibility for their children or the abandoned partner. Against this social background, Buddha asked parents to select suitable partners for their children.

People today might argue that this parental duty is no longer important, and that parents should allow their children to select their partners. We agree that today's parents do not have to select partners for their children. However, parental guidance can still be a useful contribution when children select their partners.

Parents' lack of interest in their children's selection of partners may be an obvious reason why some marriages collapse and others totter. These disinterested parents would allow their teenagers to select their spouses at will. However, unguided freedom may lead some teens to make irrational decisions. Without valuable experience, they leap to the conclusion that a person's physical attractiveness is the sole criterion for selecting him or her as a marriage partner. Soon after getting married, they realize how blind they had been. They learn that more important factors, such as their partners' attitudinal improvement and emotional maturity, deserve careful attention before one makes the decision to get married.

Parental guidance would have helped these young adults to select their partners wisely and, consequently, to minimize conflicts in their marital relationships. Their own marriages have already taught the parents important lessons. They know that the personality development of each partner would play a crucial role in making a marital partnership successful. Parents can pass such vital insight on to their children. Even though parents should not select their adult children's marriage partners, parents can enlighten their children about making the right choice.

So, Buddha's advice to parents seems very practical for today's life. Parental guidance would enrich children's knowledge about selecting right partners. Marriage is the single most important step in one's life, and parents have clear reasons to be proud of themselves if they help their children at this crucial juncture.

5. Transfer the appropriate measure of family wealth to children at the right time

Finally, Buddha asked parents to hand over the correct measure of family wealth to children. This duty may seem somewhat annoying and outdated to some parents. "It is my money, my property," they may argue. "Why should I give it to the children?" We show a natural tendency to retain everything till the deathbed rather than release it. We cling to it and take refuge in it.

Of course, Buddha did not suggest that parents should hand over everything to their children and become homeless during their later years. Instead, he suggested that parents may transfer a portion of family wealth to children at the right time. A look at Buddha's own words clarifies what he actually meant. He used the word *dayajjam* to mean the family wealth that children deserve. This word means "a portion of wealth to be given as a parental gift to children." The other key word is *samaye*, which means "the right time." Buddha suggested that parents should know the right time to hand over a portion of their family wealth to their children.

This final step suggests the completion of parental dutifulness. Having been the inspiring guidance to their children's personality development and material success, now parents complete their dutifulness in style. They hand over the wealth to their children in appropriate proportions. We have seen many parents living a relaxed life after writing their last will. They are justified in thinking, "We have fully completed our duty and have achieved the utmost success as parents."

Summary

Buddha guided his lay followers toward becoming the happiest and most successful of parents. As he explained, besides providing for the physical needs of their children, parents must play a major role in every aspect of their children's life. They should guide their children's character development and education. They should enhance their children's understanding about marriage and family life. Finally, they should hand over an appropriate portion of family wealth to children at the right time. Fulfillment of these duties would make parenthood a pleasant experience. One would think over one's achievement as a parent and derive great happiness from it. Also, dutifulness would contribute to excellent relationships between parents and children. Buddha remarked that children would show their humble gratitude to parents when parents have fulfilled their duties toward them. These positive end results would make dutiful parenthood greatly meaningful.

Chapter Eight

·····································

How to Deal with Interpersonal Conflicts

When you talk to others, you may place yourself in the following five positions: I will speak at the right time; I will present facts; I will use soft language; I will speak for the listener's benefit; I will talk with compassion.

Buddha's chief disciple Sariputta,
the *Gradual Sayings*

Solving interpersonal conflicts was as important to Buddha as establishing successful interpersonal relationships. Since Buddha's newly formed society consisted of men and women from all social categories, marked personality differences existed within that society. Consequently, interpersonal conflicts inevitably emerged among its members. Buddha, with clear vision, offered valuable support to solve, and even prevent, such conflicts. Even though these instructions were addressed to Buddha's ordained disciples, they were meant for the lay community as well. This chapter will discuss these methods that, even now, are greatly effective in dealing with the interpersonal conflicts arising in our lives.

Five steps to develop communication skills

Buddha introduced, and his chief disciple Sariputta explained, a remarkably fruitful approach to dealing with interpersonal conflicts.[1] According to this method, we need to develop a set of five communication skills. Sariputta suggested that the practice of these communication techniques would bring about numerous positive effects. Failure to follow these guidelines would cause one to regret the resulting negative consequences. Sariputta also mentioned that the speaker who failed to follow these guidelines in communication is likely to meet with resistance from those listening. Let us have a close look at the five aspects of communication skills that Buddha and Sariputta regarded as essential for handling the conflicts of daily life.

Step 1: Address the matter at the right time

Timing occupied a crucial position in Buddha's communication. He identified himself as a "speaker at the right time."[2] He repeatedly stressed that the success or failure of any communication effort would depend to a great extent upon timing. Nobody, for instance, would "roll back Buddha's Dhamma Wheel" (disturb Buddha's spreading of Dhamma) since "Buddha knew the right time to speak."[3] This statement indicates that he successfully communicated the Dhamma to his listeners because of his skill in selecting the most opportune time to speak. Sariputta's elaboration of timing as a crucial factor in solving interpersonal conflicts reiterates the same idea.

Interestingly, according to recorded evidence, Buddha, in the sixth century B.C., was the first to emphasize timing as an important factor in speech. Protagoras, a pre-Socratic Greek thinker, mentioned this concept for the first time in Western history in the fourth century B.C. Isocrates, following Protagoras, said that timing, or *kairos*, was the most important requirement for persuasion. Buddhist tradition had observed the effectiveness of this practice in communication at least a half-century before.

From Buddha's point of view, "right time for communication" contains a broad meaning. First, the listener's relaxed mental state is an important consideration. Buddha's conversation with Gotami, whose only child had died, indicates the importance of this factor.[4] Gotami took her little son to many doctors, expecting them to cure him, but everybody gave her the same answer: "The child is dead." Frustrated and distressed, she eventually visited Buddha, "the best doctor," as he was identified by society. She implored Buddha to prescribe a medication that would restore the child's health. After realizing Gotami's distress, Buddha decided not to tell her the truth right away. He knew that Gotami would resist and suffer after hearing the truth, and waited for the right time to tell her the unpleasant truth.

Psychologists confirm that a person is less likely to listen when he or she is in an unhappy mood. A teen who has just brought home an average school report may protest vehemently when a parent advises him or her to make a better effort next time. A husband or wife who comes home after a confrontation with the team leader at his or her workplace may find his or her spouse's grumbling very irritating. In contrast, an effort to communicate when the listener is in a happy mood may yield better results.

Also, Buddha paid attention to the listener's physical well-being as another necessity regarding the timing of communication. He requested his disciples to first feed a man who, despite being hungry, was eager to listen to Buddha.[5] Buddha was aware that a conversation with a hungry man would bring little benefit. The sound physical condition of the listener, on the other hand, is a requirement of mental well-being. Buddha first tended an ordained disciple who had a painful skin disease and then talked to him about the Dhamma.[6] Obviously, "right time" also signifies the time when the listener is physically well and fit.

The objective of this technique is to bring happiness and benefit not only to the speaker but also to the listener. Essentially, from Buddha's viewpoint, waiting for the right time to communicate does not mean looking for the best opportunity to manipulate the listener. The presence of a selfish motive to exploit the listener clearly contradicts Buddha's teaching. As he repeatedly stressed, the speaker should be motivated by loving-kindness and compassion, and not at all by an opportunistic motive. So, choosing the most appropriate time to speak is a communication skill that embodies great power to solve and reduce interpersonal conflicts in a relationship.

Step 2: Speak about facts

Buddha further stated that refraining from false accusation is another step to improving communication skills. This step tends to reduce the conflicts in any relationship. Sariputta explained that what the speaker should bear in mind is, "I shall speak about what has happened, not about what has not happened."[7] This skill also includes refraining from exaggeration and amplification of the listener's mistakes and weaknesses, and other forms of false accusation.

From a psychological viewpoint, people may exaggerate a person's weaknesses or mistakes mainly to gain his or her attention or to give expression to their own anger. In an effort to emphasize proper care for a baby, a wife might tell her husband, "The child got the flu because you didn't cover him properly." Trying to vent his anger, the husband might retort, "You always say the stupidest things." In the first case, what has actually happened is that the child has fallen sick with flu; the given reason for the flu is a mere assumption. In the other case, the statement is a sweeping generalization: the husband makes a general claim out of a single example. Both statements are amplifications: both persons fail to say exactly "what has happened."

The same exaggeration manifests itself in different forms and on a daily basis. A mother who sees a plate slipping through her daughter's hands might scream and say, "You never hold on to anything." A wife who reads her husband's annual checkup report might say, "You don't exercise. That is why your cholesterol is high." All these statements expand, magnify, or add assumptions to what the speaker has observed.

People sometimes speak in this manner because such language is soothing to them. They may want to relieve their emotional tension by directing a verbal attack toward the person who caused that tension. However, the most probable repercussion is the growing stubbornness of the listener, who might regard the speaker's words as a false accusation or insult. Such a reaction could hardly contribute to a healthy relationship between the speaker and the listener.

Buddha suggested that, when we present the facts without attaching our own meanings to them, we are in a better position to solve a conflict amicably. While people may find it difficult to deny facts, they may welcome assumptions as a means to resist conflict resolution. For instance, the husband in the previous example may accept the fact that he has high cholesterol but deny his wife's allegation that he does not exercise. Therefore, the best approach is to focus on his high cholesterol level and to discuss suggestions to reduce it, instead of pondering the causes. What has happened has happened. The best approach, for the sake of a relationship, is to take steps to prevent a conflict from happening again rather than to focus on how it happened.

Again, this step does not mean that if something is a fact we should always speak about it to the person concerned. Buddha said, "Even if something is true, I do not speak the truth when it is not agreeable to the listener."[8] Some truths may not serve any valid purpose, so talking about them may be useless. However, if we expect to bring about positive changes in our companions' attitudes and behavior, we must concentrate on facts rather than on assumptions.

Step 3: Use soft language

The use of soft language, according to Sariputta's explanation, signifies another important aspect of communication which successfully deals with interpersonal conflicts. Sariputta clarified that the speaker should make a firm determination about the use of language: "I should use soft words, not harsh, rough words." In fact, abstaining from using harsh language is one of the eight precepts for a lay Buddhist. This emphasis highlights the crucial role words play in our everyday relationships.

"Using soft language," as it was presented in Buddha's teaching, covers a broad meaning. It includes appropriate words, phrases, tone, and style of speech. The recurrent phrases *pharusavaca pativirato* (avoidance of harsh words) and *piya vaca* (pleasant words) indicate the very softness of the words themselves. Thus, Buddha taught that people should select pleasant words to communicate. Such phrases as *piyam vada* (speak pleasantly) and *snehena vakkami na parusena* (speak nicely, not harshly) suggest a pleasant tone and style of communication. In other words, Buddha also advised his followers to use language in a pleasant manner. The term "using soft language" includes everything related to language, such as words, phrases, tone, style, and pitch.

Illusion and anger, from Buddha's viewpoint, predominate in our minds when we use rough language as a means to solve a conflict with someone. The belief that roughness might facilitate the listener's understanding springs from illusion. The inevitable truth is that harsh language provokes the listener to resist and rebel. Some people believe that, simply because they have silenced the listener with harsh words, they have succeeded in persuading the listener to accept their suggestions. A child who remains wordless with a grim face after listening to a parent's scolding can present this false impression. In truth, however, the child's silence indicates his or her strong resistance and the parent's failure to convince the child. One who uses rough language to solve conflicts may derive immense satisfaction temporarily, but roughness would never contribute to solving a conflict.

Modern psychology explains that anger, the other forceful factor behind the use of harsh language, emerges as a reaction to a situation that would appear to be a threat. The use of angry words is a technique to destroy the source of the threat rather than to solve the conflict. In other words, angry language, tone, or style suggests an attack. The impression that the speaker is attacking with words is the worst feeling he or she can pass on to the listener. Most people do not tolerate an attack; rather, they defend themselves or counterattack. Anger-dominated harshness will rarely yield successful results in an interpersonal conflict.

Some might believe that the use of soft language reflects weakness, which a listener might take advantage of. This misunderstanding arises when softness is misinterpreted as powerlessness and timidity. The use of soft language, however, does not mean the speaker's lack of strength. Buddha constantly used soft words, but he also found emphatic language essential. Violent verbal outburst is at one extreme; powerlessness in speech is at the other. Buddha indicated that we can avoid both extremes and still use emphatic words to deal with interpersonal conflict effectively.

In the *Dhammapada*, Buddha mentioned that one should avoid words spoken in anger and rather speak disciplined words.[9] Such behavior prepares an environment that is receptive to solving the conflicts that arise in our everyday life.

Step 4: Speak with the focus on the positive effects of the solution

Sariputta further explained that the speaker needs to focus on the positive side of the suggested solution. That focus can yield great results in resolving a conflict between two closely related persons. As Sariputta instructed, the speaker needs to bear in mind, "I will speak for the benefit of the listener." This attitude of the speaker highlights two points. First, he or she should have a clear understanding about the positive consequences of the solution. Next, the speaker should essentially explain to the listener the positive effects of the solution.

This approach to conflict resolution indicates that mere criticism without a plan to help the listener will fail to resolve a conflict between two persons. Some may tend to find fault with their associates just for the sake of criticism. Recognizing this harmful habit, Buddha said, "If a certain person always criticizes a companion, that act does not show genuine friendship."[10] When the listener detects the speaker's motive, the listener instinctively tends to reject the speaker's comments. With a productive plan beforehand, the speaker can encourage the listener to be attentive.

The speaker's clarification of the positive effects of the solution further persuades the listener to accept the suggested solution. The speaker needs to explain to the listener why the problem at hand needs a solution, and how that solution would benefit the listener.

Most listeners tend to misinterpret constructive criticism when the speaker fails to clarify the objective of a suggestion. A parent who wants a teenage son to do homework would say to him, "Get off the Internet," without explaining why the son should do so. Consequently, the son would retort, "You want to use the computer." The misunderstanding arises because the speaker did not indicate the positive effects of his or her suggestion.

The speaker's attention to the positive consequences of the suggested solution eliminates such a misunderstanding and allows the listener to think about why he or she should listen. Such an atmosphere clearly facilitates a peaceful resolution to a conflict.

Step 5: Speak with genuine compassion for the listener

Finally, a compassionate attitude should dominate the entire process of communication. One who intends to solve interpersonal conflicts successfully should derive ideas, suggestions, and solutions from a compassionate heart. The speaker should make the following determination: "I should speak with a compassionate mind, not with an angry mind."[11]

The four requirements discussed in this section so far—timing, speaking about the facts, using language skillfully, and focusing on the benefits to the listener—are all rhetorical methods which are external. The compassionate attitude is the humanistic feeling, which is internal and, of course, essential.

In modern persuasive techniques, experts tend to focus mostly on the modification of external behavior. They ask us to show professionalism, or to follow certain steps that would touch the listener. For instance, we are told to listen and say "Sorry to hear about that" when someone relates a sad personal experience. Buddha went a step ahead. He wanted us to feel in accordance with what we say.

External rhetorical methods of persuasion are essential but probably inadequate techniques to modify the behavior of an individual. The danger lies in the possibility that the listener might sense the speaker's lack of feelings. The verbal message "I love and care about you, and that is why I want you to improve" contains great power to influence a person. However, our words may fail to convey this message if we lack genuine feelings of wanting to help the other.

On the other hand, we sometimes need to question ourselves about our own true intention when we communicate with others about their unskillful actions. Do we actually possess caring feelings to help them, or do we want to hurt them and destroy their self-respect? Why does a husband or a wife, for instance, always remind the spouse about a certain mistake she or he made in the past? Why do we constantly try to "correct" a certain person? Rather than having a genuine desire to help, a disguised motive for revenge might be dominant in our inner self.

In such a situation, our behavior constantly sheds light on our actual motive, persuading the listener to resist rather than to pay attention. Determination to speak with a kind heart—"I will speak with compassion, not with anger"—will inspire the positive reaction of the listener.

Exceptions

Importantly, Buddhist tradition introduced these five steps not as a perfect remedy for all interpersonal conflicts but as a way to improve skillful communication. We may use these methods to deal with most conflicts effectively, but exceptions will always exist. When Sariputta clarified to Buddha the effectiveness of this five-step process, Buddha raised the following important point:

> Still, Sariputta, even though you follow these methods of communication, some individuals may not agree with your suggestions.[12]

On the one hand, this utterance of Buddha reflects his great insight that following the five-step communication method does not solve every interpersonal conflict. The same utterance, on the other hand, invited Sariputta to explain why some people are so resistant and how we should react to these people.

In response to Buddha's remarks, Sariputta admitted that some listeners would still resist despite the speaker's use of skillful communication methods. He cited the listeners' personality problems as a clear reason for such resistance. Buddha praised Sariputta and encouraged him to promote the recommended communication techniques for the benefit of those who would be ready to listen. Significantly, Buddha's concluding remarks in this Sutta indicate that the communication methods presented by Sariputta would encourage most people, if not everyone, to deal with their conflicts peacefully.

Other suggestions

The present discussion has focused on Sariputta's clarification of Buddha's instructions for improving communication skills and successfully resolving interpersonal conflicts. While Sariputta echoed Buddha's voice, Buddha himself discussed useful tips for the same purpose. The following techniques stand out:

1. Refrain from arguing on sensitive topics

Buddha suggested that we refrain from arguing on sensitive topics in order to minimize conflicts in a relationship. He identified speculative concepts—views and beliefs that have no scientific evidence for support—as such topics. He clearly stated that he would never argue on such issues because his argumentation would provoke confrontation rather than consensus.

Buddha's conversation with Kassapa, an ascetic belonging to a different system of thought, highlights his position in this regard. Buddha maintained close relationships with teachers of other religions. He visited them regularly and had friendly conversations with them. In his conversation with Kassapa, Buddha suggested that they should discuss only the matters on which they shared similar views. He maintained that they would leave aside disagreeable topics.[13] Continuing a healthy relationship between speaker and listener would be the objective of this approach.

Instead of arguing on sensitive topics, Buddha sometimes remained silent when others introduced such topics. He maintained that silence would be better than the possible negative consequences of speaking. Sometimes he did not hesitate to agree with different views. For instance, referring to the speakers of other traditions, Buddha said that at certain points he would agree with them. He regarded a relationship as more important than an argument on ever-debatable and metaphysical topics.

However, this assertion does not mean that Buddha refrained from argument altogether, or that he asked followers never to argue. On numerous occasions, he argued convincingly against some social practices, such as social discrimination. The *Digha Nikaya I*, for instance, contains some of Buddha's most powerful argumentative speeches. In these speeches he mostly presented strong rational appeals against unjust and harmful social beliefs and practices. However, regarding sensitive personal beliefs and practices, Buddha maintained that argumentation would be useless, and even harmful, for relationships.

At present, religious, political, and some social beliefs and practices belong to this category. If a husband and a wife who practice two different religions begin to argue about their religious beliefs, the relationship will definitely suffer. Similarly, two friends trying to demean each other's social practices would pave the way for a tense and waning relationship.

Buddha suggested that, for the sake of a relationship, we need to refrain from arguing on such topics. He indicated that rational argumentation is necessary when a belief or action tends to cause unwholesome effects. However, most religious beliefs and social practices should be beneficial rather than harmful. In this situation, the best approach is not to argue against them but to show respect.

2. Understand that some aspects of behavior are unchangeable

According to Buddha, people may have to accept some less likable behavior patterns of their close associates in order to maintain healthy relationships with them. He identified most laypeople as having some sort of inner weaknesses. "A person without mental ailments is difficult to find," Buddha claimed.[14] Some of these weaknesses include people's "failure to recognize, admit, or rectify their behavior."[15] Such being the nature of some individuals, our effort to correct them would only bring disappointment and frustration. Buddha stated that some people would naturally react with anger, ill will, and aggression to a well-intended suggestion about their behavior.[16] In such a situation, the best step is to understand and accept some behavior of our associates as unalterable.

Of course, this remark does not mean that we should accept every noisome behavior of our partners or associates. As already discussed, every individual in a relationship needs to adjust his or her behavior instead of forcing the other person to accept it. However, certain individuals may exhibit some disagreeable behavior patterns that would cause no serious threat to the relationship. Accepting such behavior seems to be more realistic than trying to change it.

Buddha noted that self-adjustment is an important characteristic of a developed person. The same adjustment also seems to reduce some unpleasant experiences in a relationship. We may find it difficult to change others according to our own wishes, but we can improve our own thoughts and actions to suit others' behavior. Buddha identified people according to their personality types. Some behavior patterns are intrinsic to certain people. So, we may make a deliberate effort to be patient and tolerant when we encounter some forms of disagreeable—but nonthreatening—behavior in our close associates.

A husband's tendency to be silent and his wife's readiness to express herself exemplify the forms of behavior that demand tolerance and acceptance. She may want him to listen and give his feedback while he wants her to express her thoughts sparingly. However, if both partners understand each other's nature, they may accept the other's behavior instead of trying to change it. Constant complaints about the other person's lack of attention or self-expression may strain a relationship. Patience, tolerance, and eventual acceptance, in contrast, will tend to reduce conflicts.

3. Provide an opportunity for improvement

Forgiveness and trust in human potential characterize two of the most important teachings of Buddha. We make mistakes. Sometimes we might make serious mistakes that will affect our relationships adversely. However, Buddha urged his disciples to forgive such mistakes and to give the wrongdoer an opportunity for improvement. Such an approach will contribute to the creation of stronger relationships.

This suggestion does not mean that people must forget about all the serious wrongdoings of their spouses, friends, and other closely connected people. Instead, it means that someone's past mistakes should not cause people to condemn the person as inherently evil and incapable of having healthy relationships. We may learn from our mistakes. We have the ability to improve, and our sullied past may not count if we become better people:

> Some persons, after being indolent in the past, become vigilant and improve later. They brighten the world just as the moon does when it is released from a cloud.[17]

So, Buddha showed great confidence in human power to improve. He claimed that, even if we have wronged others in the past, we can still change, and our change can benefit others. We constantly improve through trial and error. The mistakes we made in the past will not necessarily recur in our lives after we gain knowledge and experience. Therefore, giving others a chance to improve may be a judicious approach to solving any interpersonal conflict.

This approach may be more relevant to intimate relationships than to any others. Many who are committed to a relationship expect their partners to be faithful, but these expectations do not always come true. Violation of trust is not uncommon in our society. Some may find their partners being vulnerable to sensual pleasure. The more one loves the other, the more troubling the unexpected discovery can be.

Our culture encourages us to torment the "sinners" relentlessly. However, when we allow ourselves to revel in our resentment, we inevitably force a painful end to the relationship. A more skillful approach might be to allow the other to better understand the nature of his or her wrongdoing and allow time to correct it.

Buddha explained that attraction to the opposite gender is the most powerful natural human drive. "I have seen no other sight, sound, smell, taste, or touch than that of a woman to arrest the heart of a man," he remarked.[18] A woman can also be attracted to a man in the same way.[19] In this situation, one's acting upon inherent urges may be considered natural. Nevertheless, human beings have also developed a realistic way of thinking to counter their natural tendencies. Given an opportunity, they may understand the benefits of a realistic approach to their natural urges. That understanding may enable them to correct the mistakes that damage their intimate relationships.

The most important step to correct oneself and to restrengthen a relationship is to "see the mistake as it is, accept the wrong, and to determine not to repeat it."[20] Buddha called such people *pandita*, or developed persons. He readily accepted them into his society and allowed them to have another chance for self-improvement. This example may provide a useful approach to strengthening modern relationships.

4. Seek a harmonious separation

In everything, we find exceptions. Duties and obligations, communication skills, and other techniques are meant to reduce, not to eliminate, the conflicts that might exist in a relationship. Despite a genuine effort, some may find their problems insolvable. What did Buddha say about these unhappy and unwanted relationships? How did he want his followers to react to those who are no longer close to them?

Buddha identified several factors that lead to the appropriate termination of a relationship. The other's continued wrong conduct which goes on unchecked, danger arising from the relationship, or the futility of continuing it allow a person to rightly terminate a relationship.

In any of these situations, Buddha clearly accepted individual choice as the ultimate criterion for a decision. He told his followers to retreat from an unsuitable relationship just as a king returns from a conquered land.[21] Again, he told many of his disciples to make their own decisions either to remain with him or to leave.

However, individual freedom does not allow hasty, adamant, and lopsided conclusions; rather, rational and ethical evaluations should precede any final decisions. One must make sure that one's decision will benefit, rather than adversely affect, the people involved in the relationship, including oneself. Anyone has the right to stop a relationship if the decision meets these criteria.

Buddha's advice to Upali, a follower and close companion of the Jain leader Mahavira, bears witness to this conclusion. At the request of his master, Upali visited Buddha to defeat him in an argument. However, after listening to Buddha, Upali found his teaching worthier than Mahavira's and wished to become Buddha's follower. In reply, Buddha said, "You must evaluate your decision further; it is better for a respectable person like yourself to examine and evaluate this decision."[22] After Upali assured Buddha that his decision was well-informed, Buddha allowed him to leave Mahavira and to become Buddha's follower. Rationally investigated individual choice is the key factor that determined Upali's decision.

The same evaluation is applicable to a more personal relationship as well. During Buddha's time men and women who were married left their partners and lived a secluded life in an effort to achieve self-purification. Buddha never discouraged them so long as their self-development would cause no harm to their spouses and children. For instance, he commended Ugga, a wealthy householder, for providing for the welfare and protection of his (Ugga's) wives before leaving them.[23] Obviously, Buddha did not mean that one could leave a husband or a wife in search of different pleasures. Yet, he indicated that harmonious separation from an unwanted relationship would be better than continuing with it.

Buddha also advised people about how they should react to their former friends and associates after a relationship had ended. His discussion with Kesi, a horse trainer, indicates that one should first leave aside hatred and revengeful thoughts toward former companions even if they have caused distress in a relationship. Kesi told Buddha that he (Kesi) would kill the horses that would be unwilling to cooperate in training. Buddha said in response that he should, instead, leave aside the people who would no longer be tamable or cooperative.[24]

In Buddha's teaching, one's pursuit of hatred and revenge is never encouraged even if one has been misused or hurt by another in a relationship. Baddha stated that one would never find inner peace as long as one clings to the misdeeds done by another person in the past.[25] Taking appropriate actions against misuse is always recommended in Buddha's teaching. However, as he saw it, pursuit of hatred would only aggravate the agony that has already sprung from an unhappy relationship. People make their lives miserable by dwelling on broken relationships, but they may find harmony in life by learning to forgive and forget.

Summary

Buddha and his disciple Sariputta offered their community members invaluable guidance to deal peacefully with interpersonal conflicts. The improvement of communication skills and the development of skillful attitudes and behavior are required for this purpose. Buddha emphasized that most problems arising in close relationships can be dealt with successfully through these methods. Yet, some relationships are liable to fail however hard one tries to make them work. On such occasions, separation would be the most effective way to free oneself from the burden of conflicts. One needs to regard separation not as a method of revenge, but as a step to help oneself and one's partner.

Chapter Nine

Right Attitudes and Behavior for a Successful Social Life

Buddha cordially welcomes all kinds of people. He is friendly, unassuming, and accessible to all. . . . People of all social classes respect him.

Brahmin teacher Sonadanda,
the *Dialogues of Buddha*

Besides dealing with interpersonal relationships, Buddha also guided social relationships among his lay followers. Healthy social relationships were overwhelmingly important to Buddha because he had just formed a new society. As thousands of people from all social groups earnestly sought membership in his society, Buddha strove to discover the most effective ways to maintain unity within it, as well as with other social groups. This chapter will discuss what he recommended for his followers to make their social lives happy and peaceful.

An attitudinal change and behavior development were among the key points that Buddha emphasized in order for his lay followers to establish and maintain healthy social relationships. Buddha's guidance of his disciples' social relationships may be categorized under the following seven divisions:

1. Discard attitudes and actions based on caste, race, and color

Buddha persuaded people to disregard beliefs and practices based on caste, race, and color in order to enhance their social relationships. This message indicates one of Buddha's crucial objectives. For over forty-five years, Buddha strove tirelessly to convince society that caste, race, and color should be immaterial. He made every effort to influence people's attitudes and behavior, expecting all social groups to live together peacefully.

To understand Buddha's voice and actions against caste, race, and color discrimination, first we need to look at the history of his time. Buddha's society was distinguished by its marked social differences. Social grouping in that society was predominantly based on the caste of each individual. Brahmins, the architects of the caste system, asserted that they were the most respectable persons in society. People belonging to the royal caste came second, followed by the common public and the servants.

In this social structure, people maintained unhealthy attitudes and behavior. Those in the so-called higher castes viewed others as inferior. The members of the Shudra caste, in particular, were not allowed to have any occupation other than serving the people of the three higher castes. Religious practices and intercaste marriages were also prohibited for Shudras. Consequently, arrogance and a strong sense of superiority over other social groups dominated the attitude of the alleged higher class people. Members of the so-called lower castes, in the meantime, developed a strong sense of inferiority. Obviously, these thoughts, feelings, and actions did not represent correct social attitudes or behavior for healthy social relationships.

To rectify this unpleasant situation, Buddha first encouraged society to change its attitudes. What he launched in his society was an attitudinal revolution. He persuaded people to accept that every individual was equal by birth. Also, he asserted that neither color nor wealth would change human equality. The following quotation conveys Buddha's basic message:

> I do not call one a better or a worse person because of one's birth in a high-class family. I do not call one a better or a worse person because of one's color. I do not call one a better or a worse person because of one's wealth.[1]

With this important message, Buddha presented rational and emotional arguments to influence the rigid mentality of his society. On the one hand, he appealed to the higher class people to abandon their false beliefs and wrong practices. On the other hand, he persuaded the underprivileged class to identify their rights and abilities.

Buddha argued that the prevalent social attitudes and behavior were based on social truths rather than on absolute truths. Some traditional social groups maintained that the caste system was a divine creation, but Buddha pointed out that it was a human creation. He claimed that useless and baseless social truths should give way to new truths based on rationality and humanism. "All four castes are equal in my teaching," Buddha said. "When the waters of four great rivers flow into the ocean, the water is known as ocean water. Similarly, in my society people of all castes are equal."[2]

The same assertion is applicable to racism, the inhuman practice that still exists in some societies. Buddha did not specifically mention race discrimination because racism was not an issue in his society, where whatever racial differences existed had been incorporated into the caste system. Only color discrimination, also a major component in modern racism, prevailed in that culture. Buddha's strong opposition to the caste system and to color discrimination vindicates that he was against racism as well.

So, Buddha encouraged society to reject caste, race, and color discrimination. He indicated that, no matter what their social or physical differences, everyone deserves equal rights. This attitudinal change, in turn, would naturally encourage everyone to accept and show respect to different people and, consequently, to establish healthy relationships with them.

2. Promote women's rights

Buddha also suggested that society needs to show respect toward women, welcome their intellectual skills, and encourage their leadership in social activities. This attitude and behavior, in turn, would enhance healthy social relationships between men and women.

The importance of Buddha's emphasis on women's rights can be evaluated in the light of related views held by Buddha's society. Gender discrimination was at its height during Buddha's time. Similar to most of the ancient societies, Buddha's society had suppressed female rights. Men, who held social power, regarded women as objects for sensual satisfaction, bearers of children, and caretakers of daily chores at home. In this social situation, the dignity and intellectual strength of women received hardly any attention. Buddha persuaded his society to change its attitudes and behavior toward them.

Buddha's recognition of women's intellectual strength as being equal to men's was clearly the best message to enable people to change their narrow-minded attitudes toward women. Answering Ananda's question of whether women would have the strength to achieve the highest inner purification, Buddha replied, "Yes, a woman is capable of achieving the highest result (*arahatta phala*) in the re-nounced life."[3] With this assertion, he allowed ordination for females. Similar to ordained male disciples, females also achieved the highest inner purification and earned great respect from society. This positive change was an eye-opener for people who had devalued females.

Buddha also indicated that women's own attitudes toward them-selves should improve in order for them to live with dignity. Especially, women should identify their own skills that society had suppressed. One Sutta portrayed, in the voice of Mara (death personified), the gen-eral social evaluation of women's wisdom:

> If there is any higher and rare mental achievement, it can only be acquired by skillful men, not by women who naturally have narrow skills.

In reply to Mara's sarcastic comments, Bhikkhuni Soma said:

> You may speak your words to a person who would recognize himself or herself only by gender distinction. To a person who has developed concentration, possesses wisdom, and sees truth as it is, womanhood is no barrier at all.[4]

This answer provides a lucid example of the attitude Buddha wanted women to have about themselves. They need to have great confidence in their intellectual strength, and should not allow others to devalue their skills and abilities. In brief, they should resist gender discrimination. Their own self-esteem would enable women to live a dignified life among themselves, as well as with men.

Buddha's emphasis is that society should accept the active role of women. They should no longer be confined to the home. Instead, society needs to understand that women are capable of contributing to social progress. They can serve society by choosing, amongst a host of careers, leadership in religion and society. Ordained females in Buddha's society brought about a revolutionary change in sixth-century B.C. India: they became social and spiritual leaders. People flocked to their sanctuaries for spiritual and social guidance. Women were the persuasive speakers in Buddha's society. Similar to ordained male disciples, female disciples also took Buddha's message to society. They convinced people that social changes in various sectors would be necessary for social progress. Buddha paved the way for society to accept the active and influential roles of women in various aspects of life.

In general, Buddha emphasized that people need to identify, promote, and respect women's intellectual strength, skills and capabilities, and their active role in social and religious leadership. This improvement of attitude and behavior would promote people's healthy social relationships.

3. Accept and promote social unity and togetherness, not separation

Buddha was one of the first social reformers to advocate unity and togetherness (or integration, as we call it today) in order to create healthy social relationships. Instead of letting people live within their traditional social framework, Buddha invited them to come out and mingle with everybody and to work together for common goals. He strongly believed that togetherness would enable people to leave aside social, cultural, and racial differences, and to appreciate others.

Buddha's establishment of a new society within the traditional caste-dominated culture signifies his most innovative step to promote unity among different people. He planned his society creatively. The

caste-based traditional society consisted of four groups: religious leaders, warriors, common public, and servants. Buddha also divided his
society into four sections: ordained males, ordained females, laymen,
and laywomen. He assertively and unequivocally stated that people
of all castes would be equal in his society. An ordained person from
any caste, for instance, would enjoy equal rights with all other ordained disciples. Brahmins, rulers, farmers, traders, and the tradition-
ally categorized servants enjoyed similar rights and maintained unity
and togetherness in Buddha's new society.

Within his lifetime, Buddha's new society emerged as the most
powerful social force to challenge unjust social values, attitudes, and
actions in traditional Indian society. Hundreds of thousands of people
belonging to all social groups joined Buddha's society. They lived
peacefully, discarding the differences with which they grew up.

As people of different ethnicities and social backgrounds formed
and maintained close relationships, they understood each other and
learned to leave aside prejudice and biased attitudes. As attitudes improved, behavior toward one another also improved. All members of
Buddha's society began to treat each other as human beings worthy of
respect. Buddha, both through his words and deeds, introduced integration as an innovative and very effective concept to improve people's
attitudes and behavior in social relationships.

4. Learn to respect people for their inner val-
ues and upright conduct

Having rejected all forms of discrimination based on caste, race,
color, and gender, Buddha persuaded society to respect people for their
inner values and upright conduct. This improved attitude is a crucial
factor for people to enjoy a successful social life.

The following statement summarizes Buddha's key attitude:

> One does not become a respectable person by birth. One does
> not become a disgraceful person by birth, either. One becomes a
> respectable person by action; one becomes a disgraceful person
> by action.[5]

"Birth" means caste, race, color, gender, and so on. After rejecting
such irrational criteria, Buddha identified individual action (*kamma*)
as the most important criterion that would bring a person appreciation or disrespect. "Action" denotes intention-oriented words, deeds,
and thoughts. A person whose actions are motivated by wholesome intention deserves respect. Those who act with unwholesome intention
would be liable to disgrace.

Immediately after discarding any evaluation based on caste, race,
and color, Buddha clarified his position further:

> If someone from any family refrains from destroying life,
> from taking what is not given [e.g., stealing, corruption], from
> enjoying sensual pleasure in the wrong way, from lying, from
> speaking filthy, abusive, and harmful language, and from enter-
> taining greedy, malevolent, and misleading views, that person I
> call better than others.[6]

The phrase "someone from any family" presents a broad meaning.
"Someone" can be a man or a woman, be of any age, and living in
any part of the world. "Any family" rules out the importance of caste,
race, creed, color, and wealth as a criterion to accept or reject people.
Buddha instructed society to reject these fragile measurements. He
wanted society to respect people for their wholesome conduct and
noble thoughts. Absence of "greedy, malevolent, and misleading views"
signifies inner development. Other actions given in the quotation
indicate external behavior development. A sound combination of his
or her outer adjustment and inner development is required if we are
to respect a person.

This assertion, on the other hand, does not mean that society should condemn the people who fail to be in accord with established social norms. Buddha pointed out that our social duties should include our readiness to help people understand and follow the values that would be meaningful both to themselves and to society. We must always try to understand people, show compassion toward them, and be ready to help them. However, when it comes to appreciation and respect, we may value a person who has a developed character.

So, Buddha encouraged us to depend on people's upright conduct and inner development, rather than on their caste, race, color, gender, or wealth, in order to respect them. This improved attitude would make our social relationships stable and meaningful.

5. Learn to appreciate people's skills and abilities without discrimination

Buddha's appreciation of people for their skills and abilities is another approach to enhance individual attitudes and behavior in social life. Both through words and deeds, Buddha emphasized that people ought to be appreciated and rewarded in terms of their skills. As he exemplified and instructed, caste, race, color, personal connections, or any other irrational criterion should never influence us when we appreciate people's skills and abilities.

Buddha's appointment of Sariputta and Moggallana as his two chief disciples demonstrates his admiration of people based on their skills. Moggallana had belonged to the working class before becoming a Bhikkhu and was dark in complexion while Sariputta was fair. To Buddha, their complexions were never an issue. He appointed them as his chief disciples because he knew that they were the most capable persons for the two positions.

Again, Buddha's selection of Upali as the head of all disciplinary actions in Buddha's widespread society reaffirms his steadfast position in this regard. Upali was the barber who worked for the princes in Buddha's clan. As the princes followed Buddha's footsteps to become his ordained disciples, Upali also wished to enter the Order. Not only did Buddha readily grant Upali's request, but he also guided Upali's progress in spiritual life. As time passed, Upali emerged as one of the most knowledgeable, skillful, and well-disciplined monks. When Buddha offered titles to his ordained disciples, Upali received the title of head of all disciplinary actions.

By assigning this prestigious position to Upali, Buddha provided a solid example for his community to follow. He encouraged his followers to refrain from discrimination and to grant people their due positions. Interestingly, Buddha allowed the former barber Upali to supervise the discipline of nobles, princes, and Buddha's own relatives who obtained ordination in Buddha's society.

Buddha's praise for his female disciple Kajangala gives another relevant example of how he persuaded society to appreciate people for their knowledge and skill. This example is unique because, living in a male-dominated society, Buddha stood well ahead of its social values. The following episode and Buddha's related comments are an apt example of how he persuaded society to admire the abilities of women without falling victim to gender bias.

The story goes as follows. When Kajangala conveyed Buddha's teaching to people in a remote area, people gathered at her hermitage to listen to her. Kajangala's teaching impressed the visitors, but they were not fully satisfied because of their partiality to male dominance. Eventually, Kajangala's listeners decided to visit Buddha to clear their doubts. They walked a long distance to meet Buddha and explained to him what his female disciple taught. They wondered whether a female was wise enough to teach them. After listening to the visitors, Buddha made the following comments:

> Her answer is excellent! That is excellent, householders. Kajangala is a wise woman. If you were to come to me and ask about

the meaning of this, I would give just the same explanation as
that given by Kajangala. Indeed, what you heard from her is the
right answer, and so should you bear it in mind.[7]

Gender was never a barrier for Buddha to appreciate people's
knowledge, skills, and abilities. Significantly, Buddha praised Kajangala's wisdom and skill so greatly that he identified her skill as similar to his. He urged us to cleanse our own minds from gender bias.
We must learn to disregard a person's gender, and appreciate his or
her knowledge and skill.

Overall, Buddha guided society to appreciate people's knowledge,
skills, and abilities without discrimination. Individuals need to improve their attitudes and to develop their values beyond traditional
and social truths that have no rational basis. Such an approach would
clearly facilitate our social relationships.

6. Look at different theories, views, and practices with patience, tolerance, and open-mindedness

In his endeavor to promote healthy social relationships, Buddha
also advocated patience, tolerance, and open-mindedness toward different theories and practices. As he suggested, we need to open our
minds to what others say, think, believe, and practice instead of becoming mired in a rigid belief system.

On the one hand, the scientific outlook of Buddha's teaching encouraged him to show openness to new theories. In his philosophy, no
"isms" existed: he refused to promote any speculative concepts to support people's decisions. Buddha's conversation with Vaccha, a visitor to
his monastery, confirmed his position:

> Buddha: I have seen the adverse effects of taking speculative
> views as truths, so I am not attached to any of the speculations

[that you have just mentioned].

Vaccha: Still, do you have any speculative views of your own?

Buddha: Speculative views of my own? Vaccha, I have broken free of clinging to any speculations.[8]

The Pali term Buddha used to mean "speculative concepts" is *ditthi+gata*. Any view or belief that has no evidence is a *ditthi*. *Gata* means "taken as true." When a person has internalized a speculative belief as an absolute truth, that person is identified as *ditthigata*. Buddha had freed himself from clinging to any speculative concepts, and he encouraged all his followers to do the same. This basic principle in Buddha's teaching offered his followers freedom to examine and evaluate various theories, beliefs, and practices in terms of humanistic and pragmatic values.

On the other hand, Buddha's acceptance of some alleged absolute truths as social truths further persuaded society to show openness to views, beliefs, and practices. From Buddha's viewpoint, most truths were social constructions. *Agganna Sutta* asserted, for instance, that law, kingship, and religion are all social truths created for the benefit of humankind. Human beings in their early days lived in an unorganized society with everybody having the right to punish others. In an effort to organize and regulate society, a man was selected by consensus and entrusted with the authority to punish.[9]

Similarly, unorganized ancient society so badly needed a ruler that people jointly selected a leader who was originally known as Maha Sammata, or the Great Elect. Religion came into existence as some people, disappointed with the evil deeds of the common public, started their spiritual development.[10] In brief, Buddha clearly asserted that society created truths for pragmatic reasons.

Based on these assertions, Buddha did not oppose the alteration, replacement, or modification of those truths if the proposed changes would be more humanistic and beneficial. As Buddha pointed out, those who irrationally resist such changes have taken their own concepts as absolute, unalterable, or non-replaceable truths. They belligerently claim, "Only this is the truth; all others are false," without being open to other truths.[11]

The concept of living together, for instance, would appear to someone as wrong because he or she has embraced the concept of marriage as the only truth for a male and a female to start their family life. In the teaching of Buddha, we do not find such absolute truths and ideals. Therefore, the novelty, difference, or changeability of any idea is accepted on humanistic and pragmatic grounds.

In general, Buddha advocated a patient, tolerant, and open-minded approach to different theories, views, and practices. According to his wisdom, such an approach enables us to minimize social conflicts, enhance our social relationships, and establish social unity because the supporters of new ideas would not be our antagonists.

7. Accept argument not as a weapon, but as a quest for truth

In the previous chapter, we discussed Buddha's view that those in personal relationships need to refrain from arguing on sensitive issues. The same rule is applicable to our social relationships as well. "Those who are trapped in speculative concepts argue that their views are true," Buddha stated. "However, when others refute these concepts in a gathering, anger, shame, and suffering will arise."[12] Buddha meant that we would find no benefits in using argument as a means to demolish the opposition.

Further elaborating on his position, Buddha remarked, "Whatever speech I know to be factually true, connected with the goal, but not liked by others and disagreeable to them, I do not utter."[13] These words suggest that Buddha did not want to hurt others by speaking against the views they held. Our social relationships may run smoothly when we refrain from challenging others' personal views, beliefs, and practices.

Nevertheless, as the previous chapter discussed, Buddha never encouraged us to refrain from arguing altogether. Particularly in our social life, we need to accept and practice argumentation as an effort to search for truth, not as a weapon to attack others. Especially, we need to argue using facts, evidence, and rational claims and reasons, not using mere assumptions and speculations. Also, we need to respect the convincing arguments of others.

The following speech of Buddha sheds light on this important advice. While explaining his reluctance to argue on the concept of human existence in past and future lives, Buddha said:

> When someone asks me a question about future life, I may ask the person another question about future life. When the questioner [tries to] please me with an answer, I may [try to] please the questioner with an answer [of my own]. Therefore, let us leave aside the questions related to past existence. Let us leave aside the questions related to future existence. I will tell you [what I understand as] the truth. When the cause exists, the effect comes into existence. From the arising of the cause, the effect arises. When the cause does not exist, the effect does not come to be. When the cause ceases, the effect will cease.[14]

The validity of this explanation depends on two factors. First, our own opposition to others' speculative concepts would hardly lead to an agreement; therefore, such talk is meaningless. Second, an agreeable conclusion can be arrived at only by discussing the issues that have proof. The last three lines of this quotation contain the formula of causal argument that Buddha constantly employed to strengthen his claims. He would clarify his points using evidence, facts, and empirical knowledge but would refrain from arguing on topics that had no evidence.

So, Buddha discouraged any argument on speculative concepts, but welcomed rational argumentation. Obviously, usefulness was the main criterion for selecting some topics for argumentation. The following passage shows how and why he would argue on selected topics:

> Some recluses and Brahmins are skillful, subtle, experienced
> in argumentation, and hair-splitters . . . At some points, they
> and I agree, and, at some other points, we do not. Some of the
> things they approve, we also approve. Some of the points they
> disapprove, we also disapprove . . . Therefore, let us leave aside
> those things we do not agree with [things we do not want to
> talk about]. As to those we agree with, let the wise ask questions
> about them, ask for reasons concerning them, and talk them
> over.[15]

The purpose of Buddha's argument is not a belligerent defense of
his own view or a merciless attack on the views expressed by others.
Rather, he would argue in order to find the best answers to the questions under discussion. He would be willing to admit the soundness of
opposing arguments provided that those arguments were plausible.

This personal inclination of Buddha shows us the attitude we
should have regarding controversial issues in society. We do not always
have to conform to all social truths or simply accept certain views
and actions that would appear to be unsound and unfair. The objective of an argument is to arrive at a consensus rather than to create
confrontation. Both parties, for the sake of the best possible solution
to a problem or answer to a question, should be willing to accept the
soundness of the opposite argument. This approach is another way to
enhance our social relationships.

Summary

Buddha strove to instill and enhance improved attitudes and behavior in his followers' social relationships. With his humanistic and ratio-
nalistic approach, he persuaded his listeners to abandon class, creed,
race, color, gender, and wealth as the criteria for evaluating other
individuals. He also urged his listeners to respect people for their righ-
teousness, skills, and other qualifications. Also, Buddha encouraged
people to impartially examine different views, theories, and practices.

While he preferred not to argue on highly sensitive and controversial speculations, he was well prepared for any argumentation as a truth-searching effort, not as a medium for confrontation. These are greatly effective steps to make our own social life pleasant and meaningful.

Chapter Ten

··

False Reasoning that Hinders Wise Decisions

*I have seen no other cause than
the presence of false views to block
the origination of right thoughts in
the mind and to corrupt the right
thoughts already present in the mind.
I have seen no other cause than the
presence of correct views to inspire
right thoughts in the mind and to improve the right thoughts already present in the mind.*

Buddha, the *Gradual Sayings*

Decision making is a widely discussed topic in Buddha's teaching. He talked to his lay disciples consistently about the pitfalls of decision making. He also offered them well-formulated principles to make their decisions wiser. He identified elimination of false reasoning—removal of inner viruses, in other words—as a prerequisite for preparing ourselves for rational decisions. As Buddha pointed out, our rational thinking shines forth when we find no fallacies within us. Let us now discuss Buddha's instructions on identifying and eliminating false reasoning, thus paving the way for the next chapter to elaborate on his principles for judicious decisions.

Buddha's contemporaries' views about decision making

Attention to Buddha's contemporaries' views on decision making seems necessary in order to prepare a foundation for the following discussion. On the one hand, Buddha's society witnessed the traditionalists who denied individual rights to make decisions. They claimed that tradition, divine power, religious texts, and the gurus who developed higher powers had already made decisions for people. Accordingly, society had to accept those decisions as undeniable truths.

For instance, members of the royal caste should always be rulers and warriors, never teachers of sacred texts. This rule should never be challenged because divine power and tradition had allegedly assigned the duty of ruling to the royal caste. According to the traditionalist view, individuals had no choice but to follow the decisions that had already been made for them.

On the other hand, materialists asked people to reject the traditional views about decisions and asserted that self-interest should be the main principle in decision making. They argued that, if a decision led to one's own happiness, one should never hesitate to make that decision regardless of its negative consequences for others. Some of these materialists, for instance, urged people to borrow money and enjoy life. They argued that, death being the ultimate end, self-satisfaction should be the primary goal in life. Using logic and speculative theories to support their argument, these thinkers insisted that the individual's self-interest should be the basis for decision making.

Buddha's approach to decisions

Buddha rejected both views: the traditionalist's denial of individual rights for decisions and the materialist's overemphasis on self-interest as the criterion for decisions. Instead, he introduced new principles for decision making. These principles included rationality (broad reasoning), humanism (presence of wholesome thoughts), and pragmatism (practical usefulness). Buddha clearly welcomed individual rights and freedom to make decisions, but he asserted that the decision maker should use such rights and freedom correctly. Prior to the entire process of decision making, one should make sure that no fallacies are interfering with it.

In a broader sense, the word *moha* (illusion) actually suggests the presence of fallacious argument in reasoning. This error clouds the mind, hides the truth, and makes the decision irrational and unwise. In order to judge wisely, we first need to be aware that *moha* presents a threat to making right decisions. *Kalama, Bhaddiya, Canki*, and several other Suttas presented the ten kinds of fallacies in reasoning (*moha*), that we will now consider.

Fallacy 1: Reported information is true

As Buddha observed, one of the fallacies that may affect our ability to make right decisions is the acceptance of any reported information as true. This fallacy seems to include our readiness to accept rumor, hearsay, reports, or any information coming from sources other than our own direct experience. The tendency to accept this information as truth may hinder the rational thinking needed to facilitate proper decision making.

Importantly, this statement does not mean that we should reject most reports and secondhand information in order to make rational decisions. Instead, it means that we should respond to such information cautiously, with an open mind. As Buddha explained, "What is convincingly reported may be empty, void, [and] false while what is not reported would [actually] be fact and the truth."[1] In other words, reported information may cause "twofold results," a phrase that indicates a report may be true or false.[2] Therefore, "an intelligent person should reflect" upon the possibility that the information coming from different sources can go either way.[3] Such an approach, instead of accepting or rejecting reported information altogether, would facilitate correct judgment.

We find numerous examples in society today to support the claim that unhesitating acceptance of reported information misleads people, however reliable the sources of those reports appear to be. According to some Western media sources, the allied attack on Iraq in 2003 is a blatant disregard of international law, a violation of the human rights of the Iraqi people, and a demonstration of greed and hatred. However, according to the media reports of some other countries, the same war is a genuine effort to eliminate a global threat to world peace and to liberate the Iraqi people from dreadful oppression. Obviously, both reports cannot be true because they present drastically opposite views. Acceptance of either of the two reports as true clearly tarnishes our wise judgment.

Trust in modern advertisements further authenticates Buddha's view that unreflective acceptance of reported information leads people to wrong judgments. Some products are reported to bring about miraculous effects, but the truth is otherwise. Despite the promising statements of money-back guarantees and the like, the user's experience is contrary to these claims: the products bring no result at all, or a series of unfavorable side effects follow. The wrong decision to rely on these products was motivated by the unhesitating acceptance of reported information.

Overall, reports, information, rumor, and hearsay are all likely to be influenced by bias, partiality, and ulterior motives. Buddha urged us to exercise caution while responding to any form of secondhand information. He taught that such a reaction would clearly enhance our ability to make judicious decisions.

Fallacy 2: Traditional values, beliefs, and practices are actual truths

Buddha pointed out that the acceptance of tradition as the truth and consequent submission to traditional authority would further weaken our ability to make rational decisions. As previously mentioned, he clearly stated in *Agganna Sutta* that traditional truths are historical creations. Notably, such truths as kingship, law, religion, and various other social practices and beliefs came into existence in this way. Our dependence on these traditional truths while making decisions would mean the denial of human rationality, the basic requirement for prudent decisions.

Buddha observed that the repeated recital of hymns to please various deities was one of the decisions based on this fallacy. Simply because past generations had chanted these hymns, Buddha's generation did the same without any understanding of the existence of such deities. "When a string of blind men are clinging one to the other, neither can the foremost see, nor can the middle one see, nor can the hindmost see."[4] Similarly, those who blindly followed the tradition would go around in the same circle of traditional truth, failing to see its futility.

Importantly, however, this assertion does not mean that Buddha persuaded his listeners to discard tradition altogether in order to be able to decide wisely. For instance, he remarked that parents expect their children to follow some family traditions, and children should respect that expectation.[5] Some traditional beliefs and practices, however, would require a rational evaluation before we depend on them to make important decisions. The basic lesson is that traditional authority is not an absolute truth within which we must confine ourselves while making decisions.

The following argument may elucidate the point that a decision based on traditional authority is a weak judgment:

> Hunting is a part of our tradition. We should continue it as a source of enjoyment.

In this argument we find both a claim and the reason in favor of the claim. The claim is the acceptance of hunting as a source of enjoyment; the reason is the justification of the claim by way of traditional authority. Obviously, unquestioning submission to tradition itself authenticates the claim.

Buddha explained that this kind of reasoning would fail to inject wisdom into any decision. By citing traditional authority to justify hunting as being an enjoyable activity, the speaker implies that traditional beliefs and practices are absolute truths, and thus one should adhere to them. However, from Buddha's viewpoint, historical preservation of certain actions or beliefs does not guarantee their soundness. Therefore, traditional authority should not be the sole criterion for decisions. One who looks for wise decisions should be willing to reevaluate traditional values, beliefs, and practices.

Fallacy 3: Social truths are actual truths

During Buddha's time, social authority, in addition to traditional authority, also provided a strong reason for some social groups to justify their claims. Although connected, social authority differs from traditional authority. As discussed above, those who supported traditional authority asserted that a view, belief, or social practice was true or false because tradition accepted it. Advocates of social authority claimed that something would be right or wrong because society in general accepted it as such. They cited social authority in various terms such as "because they say so," "because that is the truth," and "because that is how it should be."

The young Brahmin Vasettha, in his conversation with Buddha, revealed one such predominant social truth in Buddha's society. Vasettha had become a follower of Buddha, but his fellow Brahmins would not tolerate Vasettha's transformation. They criticized him, saying, "Such a course is not acceptable; it is not proper."[6] They further remarked that a Brahmin, who belonged to the so-called highest social class, should not learn under the guidance of Buddha, a member of the ruling class.[7]

In this example, the truth held by some Brahmins—that a Brahmin should not study under a ruler—is a social truth, or a belief commonly held by a social group or the entire society. Of course, these truths were empowered by tradition, but social acceptance was the underlying reason to support these claims.

Buddha identified dependence on social authority as a crucial obstacle to wise decisions. Referring to Vasettha's remarks mentioned above, Buddha noted that an evaluation of the historical development of the Brahmin view would confirm its falsity. He instructed his community to reject social authority, which is "just a sound of the world," as termed by Buddha's disciple Kaccana.[8] The Pali term *ma itikiraya* (*ma*: do not accept/take; *itikiraya*: [because] thus it is said/accepted as true), means that social acceptance or rejection is not a dependable reason for us to accept or reject something.

For many people today, submission to social authority is a powerful hindrance to wise decisions. Social truths are so powerful that we tend to take them as true not because they contain rational value but because society in general accepts them as true.

A high schooler, for instance, would argue, "I should have the right to make my own decisions because that is how it should be, and that is what my friends do." A parent, on the other hand, would dispute this argument, saying that a child should always follow the advice of parents because "that is the right way." Obviously, both arguments are based on social authority. The teen echoes submission to the predominant power in his or her own social group. The parent exhibits wholehearted acceptance of the truth within his or her own social circle. Both the child and the parent fail to evaluate the other person's view rationally because both have become victims of social authority. This example clarifies how surrender to social authority prevents people from making correct decisions.

Interestingly, social truths seem to be actual truths even though they are not. Social truths are so powerful that, unless we are mindful of their strength, they quickly invade our minds and overpower us. Buddha advised us not to fall prey to irrational social truths in order to retain our ability to make correct decisions.

Fallacy 4: Texts are true

Submission to textual authority is another pitfall that Buddha identified as an obstruction to our rational decisions. The Vedic tradition during Buddha's time consistently used textual authority to strengthen such beliefs as divine creation of a caste system and divine assignment of duties to each caste. Advocates of the Vedic tradition argued that society should accept these concepts as absolute truths simply because they were accepted in sacred texts. Buddha strongly challenged this argument. He asserted that a decision based on textual authority would fail to support the decision maker's wisdom.

Buddha stated that the so-called sacred texts were a human creation. This statement makes Buddha the first thinker to claim that religious truths are social constructions. As he explained, after ancient Brahmins began their religious practices, they started preparing texts.[9] Therefore, the so-called absolute truths presented in those texts could be erroneous. The decisions based on such texts could also be wrong.

Societies still tend to use texts, particularly religious texts, as a dependable criterion for decision making. Consequently, people may arrive at conclusions that are dubious and devoid of rationality. Abortion, homosexuality, and same-sex marriage are some of the popular topics regarding which textual authority comes to the forefront.

The argument in favor of male dominance in marriage is a clear example of how textual authority tends to challenge human wisdom:

Claim: A wife should always make her husband happy.

Reason: Because she was created by God to help man get rid of his (man's) loneliness.

Perhaps this argument is less obvious in mainstream American culture. However, other societies, as well as some minority groups in America, still use this argument, perhaps tacitly, to protect male superiority in marriage. The use of textual authority as a reason to support this argument clearly makes the claim very fragile. The given reason is merely a textual speculation that has no evidence at all. We sacrifice rationality and the humanistic value of a decision when we surrender to textual truths that have been created to influence ancient cultures.

To Buddha, texts were never a reason to justify a claim since a decision based on mere textual authority would not reflect the decision maker's wisdom. Rejection of textual authority, according to Buddha, is a clear sign of arriving at wise conclusions.

Fallacy 5: Logical reasoning is always correct

Buddha used the word *takka* for the kind of logical reasoning he wanted his followers to be cautious about. "Trick," the English derivation of this word, tells it all. Dependence on some kinds of logical reasoning can mislead the thinker. In modern argumentation, most of these tricks, or flimsy forms of reasoning, are identified as logical fallacies.

Dependence on enticing but shallow logical analogies is one form of logical reasoning that Buddha identified as obstructive to clear thinking. During Buddha's time, certain thinkers used such analogies to support their views. The following comparison given by Makkhali Gosala, a famous thinker of the time, is an apt example:

> When one flings a bundle of string while standing on the top of a mountain and keeps hold of one end of the string, the spool goes down to its end and then stops. Similarly, every person will continue to be born in a certain number of lives after death, and then his or her existence will cease.[10]

Even though at first sight this statement seems logical, a closer observation demonstrates that the comparison is senseless and empty. Basically, we find no connection between a bundle of string, which is a visual object, and rebirth, a metaphysical concept. A spool of string that rolls down a mountain does not provide evidence to support the claim of rebirth. In fact, the comparison is a trick to strengthen the claim that an individual continues to be reborn a certain number of times. We fail to decide wisely if we take this logical comparison for granted.

The following conclusions exemplify several other kinds of logical reasoning that Buddha recognized as an obstruction to rational thinking:

> These ascetics are well disciplined. They have achieved enlightenment.[11]
>
> His ancestors on both his mother's and father's sides have been Brahmins. Therefore, he is a noble person.[12]
>
> If Buddha performs a miracle, Buddha can prove his status as an enlightened person.[13]

In the first example, Buddha remarked that the reason was inadequate to support the claim. One would have to examine the ascetics more closely in order to find out whether or not they were enlightened. In the second argument, the given reason, according to Buddha, was irrelevant because he found no relationship between one's having Brahmin ancestors and one's being a noble person. The reason in the third argument is totally unrelated to the claim because Buddha saw no connection between one's achievement of enlightenment and one's ability to perform miracles. Adherence to these logical fallacies clearly hinders one's rational judgment.

The following argument provides a relevant example of how dependence on this type of reasoning can lead us to irrational conclusions in our daily life:

> Look at his beat-up car. He must be very poor.

This conclusion may be erroneous because of several reasons. Prosperous people may prefer old cars in order to deter criminals. Others would have old automobiles purely because simplicity suits their lifestyle. In fact, research has revealed that an increasing number of wealthy people tend to live a simple life rather than display their material possessions; therefore, driving an old car does not necessarily attest to one's poverty. This example elucidates Buddha's point that one who depends on logic might fail to decide wisely.

Still, Buddha's warning about logical reasoning does not mean that he urged society to reject logic altogether. His advice was that one should be cautious about the fallacies associated with logic. On various occasions Buddha used logical argumentation to strengthen his claims and to counter the opposition. Nevertheless, he made it clear that total dependence on logic may prevent people from arriving at rational conclusions. The following words of Buddha make this point more explicit:

> One who uses logic may argue correctly or incorrectly; the argument may be so or otherwise. Therefore, a wise person should reflect thus: "This person uses logic to investigate. Logic may be correct or incorrect; it could be so or otherwise."[14]

What Buddha emphasized throughout his speeches was that experience and understanding, rather than logical assumptions, would provide the key to wisdom. We need to evaluate logical assumptions cautiously and give priority to our own experience and wisdom in order to decide the rightness or wrongness of any action.

Fallacy 6: Reasoning based on imagination and speculation is correct

Buddha further clarified that the acceptance of reasoning originating in imagination and speculation can lead us to unwise decisions. The following view held by the Brahmin tradition in Buddha's time is a prime example of this error:

> A member of the Shudra caste must serve the other castes because Brahma created the first Shudra from his (Brahma's) feet.

The conclusion that Shudras should be servants is based solely on the imagined and speculated theory that the first Shudra was born from the creator's feet. In this argument, a Shudra is low in status because Brahma's foot is an unsuitable source for a human being. Buddha stated that one's acceptance of this claim is not a wise judgment because the reason given in favor of the claim is merely speculative.

The words "imagination" and "speculation" seem to need more attention in this discussion. Basically, we find two kinds of theories in society: one based on reasoning and knowledge and the other on imagination and speculation. For instance, the Theory of Evolution is said to depend on knowledge and reasoning while the Theory of Creation is based on imagination and speculation. While Buddha did not want his lay community members to cling to any kind of theory, he specifically persuaded them not to depend on speculative and imaginary theories for decision making.

Still, Buddha encouraged his society to respect rational theories for decisions. In *Agganna Sutta*,[15] he considered the social differences between people and concluded that social evolution could be the reason for such differences. As he noted in the same Sutta, the caste system was a social creation. He then used the concept of social evolution to make the following conclusion:

> People of all castes should have equal rights because the caste system that led to discrimination was a human invention, not an actual truth.

This example and many others make it clear that Buddha regarded rational theory to be important in decision making. Despite his cautious approach to all theories, Buddha respected the rationality behind a theory as a means to facilitate a wise decision. At the same time, he strongly opposed submission to speculative theories when making decisions.

People still hold on to speculative theories, and, consequently, tend to make irrational decisions. The following argument provides an example:

> The creator welcomes a suicide bomber who destroys enemies; therefore, a suicide attack to kill enemies is justifiable.

In this argument, the decision to kill oneself and others is based on the speculative theory of creation and its related concepts; therefore, that decision is clearly unwise. The problem in this argument, as well as in any argument based on imagination and speculation, lies in the fact that no evidence is available to support the claim. The existence of a creator cannot be proved, so the claim of the creator's open arms for a suicide bomber is totally irrelevant.

Buddha's definition of speculative theories further clarifies the absence of evidence for these theories. As he termed it, speculative theories are "hammered out by one's own line of thought."[16] Conceived through mere brainstorming, such theories follow their inventors' speculative skill, not true knowledge. Thus, decisions based on imagination and speculation fail to demonstrate our prudence.

Fallacy 7: Hypothesized reasoning is correct

Dependence on hypothesized reasoning, according to Buddha's observation, is another barrier to wise decisions. Those who depend on this sort of reasoning find quick and easy answers to complex problems. However, these answers and solutions are often unrealistic, impractical, and devoid of rationality so that a decision based on hypothesized reasoning reflects little wisdom.

The following argument presented by some people in Buddha's society exemplifies hypothesized reasoning:

> Those who belong to a lower social class by birth are incapable of achieving the mental development necessary for holy life. Therefore, people of the low classes should not be allowed to enter holy life.[17]

Highlighting the weakness of this argument, Buddha asked, "On what strength and authority do they speak thus?"[18] In other words, the statement that people in some social groups are inherently incapable of achieving mental development has never been tested or proved. The so-called pundits, resting comfortably in plush chairs, may indulge in this type of reasoning, but it is far from the truth.

Through his own actions, Buddha demonstrated that a decision based on this fallacious reasoning is devoid of rational thought. For instance, he ordained many people belonging to lower social classes, and helped them achieve success in their spiritual lives. By doing so, he disclaimed the view that only people of higher classes could achieve progress in spiritual life and become successful social campaigners.

Traditionalists in Buddha's society used the word *parisuddha* (purification) to mean spiritual progress. Referring to this word, Buddha humorously remarked that, similar to a person in a higher class, any individual could step into a bath with soap and a scrub brush to "purify" himself or herself. Buddha thus refused to accept hypothesized reasoning as a criterion for decisions.

We may cite the following example as a classic modern illustration of hypothesized reasoning:

> Question: Why do some people fail to succeed even though they try hard?
> Answer: Because of their bad luck.

The so-called bad luck may be attributed to a fall from divine grace, negative influence of planets, or unwholesome Karmas of past lives, yet all of these reasons are mere hypotheses because they have no evidence. The actual reasons may go unnoticed as we tend to use hypothesized reasoning. In the given example, for instance, people do not become successful through hard work alone. As Buddha himself suggested, they need to make rational decisions, plan well, and get organized. Many also struggle for success because failure is an inevitable outcome of the capitalistic economic system. Dependence on hypothesized reasoning prevents us from discovering the real reasons why some fail despite their perseverance.

Buddha's rejection of hypothesized reasoning, on the other hand, does not suggest that hypotheses are useless for rational decisions. Of course, we often hypothesize as a preparation for making decisions, but even a seemingly valid hypothesis can turn into utter falsehood when we continue to examine it. In other words, hypotheses may not be true because, by definition, they are only guesses. Buddha's advice is that we need to examine our hypotheses closely in order to determine their soundness.

Fallacy 8: One should accept a view because it is compatible with one's own way of thinking

Buddha identified the "because I like/don't like it" approach as a hindrance to wise judgment. People exhibit a tendency to embrace views simply because these views correspond with their own way of thinking. In this situation, they actually approve of their own view rather than of somebody else's. Such an approach, according to Buddha, fails to reflect the wisdom of the decision maker.

The reaction of the ascetic Keniya after he listened to Buddha is a relevant example of how this fallacy may prevent one from making rational decisions.[19] Keniya visited Buddha to learn the Dhamma, and the text indicates that Buddha gave an enlightening talk to his visitor. In honor of that speech, Keniya invited Buddha and his disciples to visit his residence for a meal. Nevertheless, Keniya failed to accept Buddha's reasoning because he (Keniya) was "pleased enough to believe what he heard from Brahmin teachers."[20] In other words, Keniya indicated that he did not want to reject what he liked even though Buddha's counter-argument exposed the irrationality in Keniya's inclination.

Notably, this fallacy constantly leads an individual toward wrong decisions in daily life. Most judgments based on mere individual preference fall into this fallacy. Those who use this fallacious reasoning may support their claims with the following reasons:

> Because I like/don't like/hate it
> Because I want/don't want it
> Because I think/don't think so

Of course, individual freedom to make decisions is a distinguishing characteristic in Buddha's teaching, but mere individual preference is not. In other words, Buddha asserted that, in addition to considering our own strong inclination toward a certain decision, we also need to evaluate other reasons. The next chapter will discuss this topic in detail, but basically, mere individual choice failed to win Buddha's appreciation as a wise criterion for decisions.

Upon further examination, we find that individual fondness for a certain decision connects to naturalism while readiness for further evaluation of the possible consequences of the same decision relates to rationality. Nature has given human beings a powerful urge for certain actions. Yet, putting such an urge into action without evaluating its possible effects can cause huge damage. The "because I like it" approach to justify an action touches the natural instinct of the human being, a tendency that ignores the repercussions of a particular action. This point further highlights the danger of a decision that is merely motivated by the individual's inner propensity.

As Buddha pointed out, desire for sensory satisfaction naturally predominates over all human behavior. In this situation, people may find many attractive views, ideas, and practices that are compatible with their way of thinking. However, Buddha made it clear that submission to such natural urges would not bear witness to the decision maker's wisdom. A wise person would be patient enough to evaluate other reasons rather than surrender to his or her own inner tendency.

Fallacy 9: One's persuasive skill validates the message

This fallacy means that a person who is capable of presenting an idea skillfully is also presenting the right idea. Buddha encouraged his listeners to reject this criterion. Even though someone appears to be very skillful in persuasion, he or she may not convey the right message. Consequently, our trust in such a person may not always lead us to right decisions. In other words, we should not allow other people's persuasive skill or rhetorical authority to dominate our conclusions.

In his society, Buddha found many people striving to influence the decisions of an enthusiastic audience. These persuaders, who argued on various topics related to religious, social, and spiritual matters, used their argumentative power and rhetorical skill to influence people. They spoke fluently, defeated opponents, and appealed to the audience in a convincing way. Some of them were very famous, and victorious in most of their debates with opponents. Saccaka, for instance, was such a winner who boasted, "Even a lifeless wooden post would tremble and shake when I challenge it with my words; so why should a human being not!"[21]

Buddha reminded his community to be cautious about the correctness of the messages even though the debaters defended their views successfully. He implied that the claim and the reason in each of the following examples do not match:

> She silenced her opponents; her point is correct.

> The candidate made a beautiful speech on his policies; he will become a successful leader.

In the first sentence, the speaker's ability to silence the opposition justifies the claim that the speaker's argument is correct. Yet, one's ability to defeat the opposition in an argument does not mean that one's argument is correct. Perhaps the winner is more skillful in debating, and the loser may have failed to make his or her point clear. Perhaps the winner has mastered the art of argumentation, and the opponent therefore failed to gain the upper hand in a verbal battle. In these situations, the winner has impressed the audience not because his or her argument proved itself to be correct but because the winner's argumentative skill dominated the loser.

The second example makes the same fallacy even more obvious. The ability to make a successful speech on policies does not necessarily confirm the candidate's ability as a leader. On the one hand, someone else could have prepared the speech for the speaker; some politicians, in particular, often operate this way. On the other hand, even if the speech is truly a product of the speaker, we may still find very little connection between a person's ability to prepare and present a successful speech and his or her capability as a leader. Therefore, the reason given in the second example does not clearly support the claim. Both examples illustrate Buddha's points that one's argumentative skill does not always validate a message, and that the listener should not always favor the winner.

The phrase "persuasive skill" includes not only the speaker's argumentative skill but also his or her rhetorical tactics. One who makes rational decisions should not become a victim of these tactics. Buddha was very much aware of these techniques when he recognized right timing and right understanding of the audience as the requirements for persuasion. Skillful persuaders—or manipulators, as they are best termed—may select the most appropriate time to dupe us into making unwise decisions. Buddha guided us to be mindful about these tactics.

This statement, on the other hand, does not mean that rhetoric fails to lead people to right decisions. As Buddha emphatically stated, rational argumentation always leads to right conclusions. Buddha's concern, instead, related to manipulation by skillful persuaders who used various rhetorical techniques to present themselves as the most capable people to lead society into making right decisions. These apparently capable but actually deceptive individuals strengthen their claims by way of their rhetorical skill. However, the listener should always be mindful that the speaker's rhetorical skill alone will not lead one to wise decisions.

Fallacy 10: Individual authority is a dependable criterion for making decisions

Buddha also maintained that submission to individual authority could obstruct our ability to make wise decisions. Both this fallacy and the one discussed above do have close links, but they differ in the following way. While rhetorical authority specifically focuses on one's ability to manipulate the listener through rhetoric, individual authority emphasizes the power behind one's personality. Society may tend to accept the views and respect the guidance of those who have or seem to have strong personalities. According to Buddha, however, this social attitude is not necessarily correct.

Many components combine to enhance the power of personality in different individuals. Characteristics, knowledge, social status, experience, skill, appearance, and apparent qualifications play a major role in constructing a strong personality. Such a personality seems to have magical power: it possesses enormous ability to influence. Buddha noticed the danger lurking behind individual authority. He observed the possibility that those who truly possessed a powerful personality, as well as those who professed to possess it, might lead society to arrive at the wrong conclusions.

The following examples show how influential people in Buddha's society displayed personal authority to influence others:

> 1. Brahma revealed to me that the caste system is a divine creation. Therefore, you should not challenge the caste system.

> 2. After developing the mind through strenuous effort, I realized that Karma is unchangeable. Therefore, you have to accept your destiny.

> 3. He is a student of a distinguished teacher. He has acquired all the knowledge required to be a teacher. So he is capable of teaching you the right practice.

The assumed strength in each of these examples is individual authority: divine favor in the first, self-realization in the second, and social status and self-fulfillment in the third. The authority expressed in the first two examples is questionable: nobody knows or can test whether the asserted authority is true. In the third example, the authority may be true or, at least, can be checked. Overall, all the claims in the given sentences depend on individual authority, either pretended or actual.

Buddha warned that we would find no way to make sure that the self-proclaimed authority in the first two examples was genuine. Even though the authority given in the third example might be true, that authority does not guarantee the speaker's ability or the genuine intention to lead the listener along the right path. Therefore, to decide wisely, the listener should first make the following inquiries:

Is the alleged authority real?

If it is real, does the authority justify the person's ability?

Is the authoritative person sincere in his or her motives?

In one of his remarkable statements, Buddha asked Upali, a businessman who was willing to accept Buddha as his new spiritual leader, to make a deeper inquiry about Buddha and his teaching.[22] Such an inquiry would enable Upali to select his leader wisely. Confidence in a person who falsely claims to have qualifications and abilities may lead us to make irrational decisions.

Importantly, this advice of Buddha does not suggest that the ideas of an authoritative person should be rejected. In several speeches, Buddha stressed that one should rely on personal authority only after a thorough investigation. According to many of his speeches, we should turn to the authoritative people in a particular field instead of making our own uninformed decisions. One should first be convinced that the alleged authority is true, and that the authoritative person possesses the ability and the intention to guide one along the right path.

Combination of false reasoning

Buddha also noticed that some of his contemporaries used several of these fallacious reasoning methods to heighten their claims. For example, some traditionalists used reports, individual authority, logic, and snap reasoning to amplify the claim that they were superior to other social classes. In his conversation with Bharadvaja, a young Brahmin who was interested in Buddha's teaching, Buddha took each of these fallacies for analysis, saying, "First, you cited individual authority, and now you are talking about the authority of the report."[23] Buddha examined each of these fallacies to show how misleading they could be. Then, he concluded:

> For a wise person who strives to discover and preserve the truth, this [the use of fallacious reasoning] is not sufficient to decide that something is the truth, and others are false.[24]

We observe that some social groups at present extensively use a combination of false reasoning methods to add more power to their claims, and, of course, they succeed occasionally. The claim that people should fight for the sake of religion is an example in this regard.

Textual, traditional, and social authorities would be the reasons in favor of this claim.

Just one kind of drug impairs a sober individual, but a cocktail has devastating effects. Similarly, a single form of false reasoning may affect a person's wise judgment, but a combination, if accepted unquestioningly, would hypnotize the person and paralyze his or her mind. We use the word "brainwashed" to identify the mental status of a person who has fallen prey to various forms of false reasoning.

This mental degeneration, the ultimate outcome of one's total surrender to several forms of authority, suggests refusal to make independent decisions. In this extreme situation, the victim turns out to be a puppet who depends on fallacious arguments for guidance.

Most of the dictators in the past, for instance, persuaded their societies to rally behind them not because they conveyed the right message but because they effectively brainwashed an entire society with a combination of their rhetorical skill and individual authority. Vicious leaders who persuade people to launch suicide attacks also use a host of fallacies to nullify the right thinking of their followers. All these examples illustrate Buddha's point that unconditional submission to various forms of authority and fallacious argumentation persuades people to depart from wisdom and to arrive at unwise decisions.

How to break the cage and explore the beautiful world

When Buddha explained to Bharadvaja that false reasoning would lead an individual toward wrong decisions, the latter made the following request:

> To what extent, sir, does one see the truth? What awakens one to the truth? We are asking Buddha about awakening to the truth.[25]

The detailed answer Buddha gave to this question should stand as timeless guidance to relieve an individual from the burden of false reasoning. Those who preserved this Sutta seem to have reorganized its content, but the basic steps to a balanced reasoning remain intact. In this speech, Buddha first identified self-imposed imprisonment within one's own mental world as the worst hindrance to liberation from false reasoning. He then introduced several useful steps to find inner freedom. Having a desire for learning, striving for the truth, listening, approaching, testing what is learned, and weighing the different views and practices are some of the interrelated steps that would help one eliminate false reasoning.

These suggestions deserve more attention in order to clarify their effectiveness. Buddha always recognized the human capacity for self-improvement, and one's ability to eliminate false reasoning is a relevant example. However, if a person tends to close his or her mind only to take refuge in the fallacies embodied within it, he or she would find no way to escape. Essentially, interest and readiness are the most important prerequisites to the freedom of thought. Buddha noted that desire within the individual would serve as a forerunner to effort, the next step for advancement. Contrary to some people's opinions, Buddha actually taught about individual need and inner desire:

> Need provides great help for effort. If need does not originate within, one will not make an effort. If desire does originate within, one will make an effort. Therefore, desire is extremely helpful for effort [to find the truth.][26]

So, Buddha persuaded us to show an interest in the wide world of ideas, views, and practices as a preparation for the elimination of false reasoning. Once the seed of interest germinates and sprouts inside, the mind would naturally tend to search, investigate, compare and contrast, and, eventually, select wise criteria for decisions. As Buddha observed, searching, approaching, listening, testing, and weighing the different truths would pave the way for interested individuals to select advanced criteria for decision making.

Some might believe that the inability to depart from logical fallacies is an inherent weakness in certain individuals. Nevertheless, we
observe the soundness of Buddha's claim that, with interest and effort,
people tend to shatter the fetters of false reasoning. In closed societies,
an overwhelming majority of people continue to depend on fallacious
reasoning because they do not find the resources to kindle their interest in different views. Even though such resources are amply available
in some open societies, people may still be reluctant to examine the
wide world of ideas, views, and practices. In such situations, people inevitably fail to understand the hollowness of fallacious reasoning.

Buddha's message to those who entertain various forms of fallacies
is an optimistic one. He stated that individuals possess the potential to
emerge from fallacious argumentation. Openness, which permits the
influx of different views, is a welcome way to realize this potential. As
our horizon broadens, we discover better and more profound reasons
to defend or refute a multitude of thoughts and actions.

Summary

Buddha identified fallacious reasoning as a formidable threat to
rational thinking. Blinded by numerous fallacies, most people fail to
show wise judgment in their decision making. Altogether, Buddha
recognized ten fallacies that constantly spring up in our minds to
thwart the wisdom behind our decisions. While each of these fallacies
may work alone, sometimes they combine and disturb our judgment.
Elimination of fallacious reasoning is the gateway to wise decisions.
Openness to different views and ideas is an effective step to free ourselves from false reasoning. Fallacies tend to lose their firm grip on
our minds as we continue to examine the wide world of ideas.

Chapter Eleven

Correct Reasoning for Wise Decisions

If you understand that this action is right, harmless, blissful, beneficial, and admirable, take that action and follow it.

Buddha, the *Gradual Sayings*

As Buddha discussed in several of his speeches, elimination of fallacious reasoning is just the beginning for making rational decisions. After getting rid of the fallacies discussed in the previous chapter, we still need to follow a guided process in order to arrive at the most appropriate decision. To facilitate the discussion of that process, let us first look into the mental status of the individual who has bid farewell to various forms of false reasoning. We will then discuss what Buddha considered as the correct or true evaluation that would actually lead us toward correct decisions.

Importantly, by helping us to eliminate false reasoning, Buddha strove to secure a crucial necessity for right decisions: inner freedom. He meant that the various forms of fallacious argumentation discussed in the previous chapter tend to restrict our mental capacity and disturb our reasoning power. When these agents no longer interfere with our decisions, we find no limitations in our rational thinking. Mental freedom results when we give up fallacious reasoning as the criteria for our decisions. Buddha encouraged us to reject fallacious reasoning as a means of accommodating freedom of thought.

We need to exercise extreme caution while discussing Buddha's concept of inner freedom. The absence of fallacious reasoning for decisions, according to Buddha, does not mean the presence of the right to do anything we want. Instead, by helping to eliminate false reasons, Buddha paved the way for us to travel beyond social, cultural, religious, and intellectual restrictions. He urged us to examine the other reasons for our decisions and to *know* why we should make, or refrain from making, certain decisions. "Know" is the key word. Buddha offered us unrestricted freedom to examine and know why a certain decision is right and another wrong.

Referring to a person's intended decision, Buddha repeatedly mentioned that knowledge would allow the person to decide correctly. While some contemporary teachers cited beliefs and social practices to justify their claims, Buddha often asked, "Do they *know* their point as

true and others' points as false?"[1] Again, immediately after he rejected
various methods of false reasoning, Buddha encouraged his listeners to
make the right choice based on knowledge, understanding, and wisdom.

"Know by yourself" is the term that clearly indicates Buddha's
point.[2] He asserted that one's acceptance or rejection of ideas and
practices should depend on right knowledge. Undoubtedly, freedom to
seek knowledge is the highest blessing that we may secure after putting aside fallacious reasoning.

The word "knowledge" may need further explanation. Blinded by
false reasoning, some may see an assumption, hypothesis, intuitive
urge, or hallucination as knowledge. However, as Buddha specifically
and unequivocally stated, knowledge means right understanding with
evidence. The following dialogue between Buddha and his visitor Bharadvaja clarifies what Buddha specifically meant by knowledge:

> Bharadvaja: Referring to the ancient mantras that come from
> oral tradition and textual preservation, some assert, "These are
> true; anything else is unwise." What do you, sir, say about this
> [argument]?
> Buddha: What do you say about this [question], Bharadvaja?
> Among these teachers, is there at least a single person who can
> say, "I know and I see these mantras as true, and anything else
> is unwise"?[3]

This example and many others confirm that knowledge, according to
Buddha, can be obtained with direct experience and evidence. Traditionalist teachers failed to recognize their mantras as true because
their own experience gave them no evidence to support their claim.
Again, according to *Vasettha Sutta*, the concept of Brahma presents itself to be false because nobody has sensually experienced the existence
of Brahma.[4] Overall, knowledge means clear and reliable evidence,
particularly the evidence obtained through direct experience. To make
the correct decision, we need to have knowledge about everything related to that decision.

Kalama Sutta **as an important source of right knowledge for decisions**

Kalama Sutta has summarized one of Buddha's most comprehensive discussions about knowledge. After identifying the fallacies in argument, this Sutta elaborated on what kind of knowledge would be necessary for a person to make the most appropriate decisions.

As discussed in Chapter One, the members of the Sangha community preserved the huge collection of Suttas through memory. In this process, they condensed Buddha's long speeches to a minimum for the sake of preservation. *Kalama Sutta* seems to be one of Buddha's speeches that went through rigorous summarization. In particular, the section that refers to knowledge about decisions appears to be a detailed explanation by Buddha. However, this section now contains only two paragraphs. Despite its brevity, the related section in *Kalama Sutta* clearly guides us toward the correct knowledge required for judicious decisions. Along with several other discourses, this speech presents a clear picture of what Buddha meant by "right knowledge" about decisions.

Kalama Sutta offered four forms of correct evaluation, all based on knowledge and understanding, to lead us toward right decisions. We should apply all four criteria in order to make a single wise decision. Let us take each of these evaluations for a detailed discussion.

Right Evaluation 1: Wrong motivations lead to wrong decisions

Buddha claimed that, when a wrong inner urge motivates a person, the decision that follows fails to reflect the decision maker's wisdom. Altogether, Buddha recognized three such motivations: greed, malice, and illusion. Of course, these three motivations are the most common of all human motivations, but, as Buddha explained, they all can easily corrupt a decision.

In the previous chapter, we discussed how illusion, the third motivation given above, tends to remove wisdom from a decision. There, we saw illusionary views restricting the individual's inner freedom and suppressing his or her rational thinking. In the present section, we will elaborate on how greed and malice, the other two motivations, tend to hamper the wisdom of the decision maker.

How greed affects a decision adversely

To clarify how greed tends to make a decision unwise, we first need to have a clear picture of what "greed" means. For the reader's convenience, we have to select English equivalents for Pali terms while discussing Buddha's teaching. Although the word "greed" serves that purpose, it fails to convey what Buddha meant by several Pali words, which, of course, connect to, but go beyond, what we mean by greed.

On different occasions, Buddha used such words as *lobha, raga, tanha,* and *mahaiccha* to mean this unwholesome motivation. *Lobha* may be defined as insatiable desire for material objects or power. *Raga* basically refers to the desire for bodily satisfaction. *Tanha* means "the desire for possession and sensory satisfaction." *Mahaiccha* seems to suggest thinking and desiring beyond one's needs. The word "greed" includes all these meanings. Buddha meant that these different aspects of greed clearly obstruct human wisdom in a decision.

Obviously, uncontrolled desire for sensory satisfaction leads to irrational and harmful behavior. As a result, decisions made in a greedy spirit reveal no wisdom on the part of the decision maker. Wrongful conduct, or *kamesu micchacara,* is the next reaction of the greed-dominated person. This reaction would almost always lead to unwholesome effects. "I have seen nothing other than greed to cause so many damaging effects," Buddha once observed. "Greed is very harmful."[5]

Identifying some of these negative consequences, Buddha again noted, "*Tanha* breeds sadness and suffering; *tanha* breeds fear."[6]

Blinded by the burning desire to satisfy both body and mind, a greedy person may take falsehood as truth and make decisions that are devoid of wisdom. He or she fails to realize that suffering would be the eventual outcome of greed-motivated decisions. Clarifying Buddha's teaching, his disciple Ananda remarked that, driven by greed, one would fail to differentiate between what is beneficial and what is harmful.[7] This weakness of the greedy person makes his or her decisions injudicious.

Violent actions and destructive, merciless behavior kindled by hunger for power demonstrate how greed further affects decisions. "The greedy thought, 'I will become powerful; power is important to me,' produces numerous evil and unwholesome effects," Buddha explained. "Overwhelmed by greed and devoid of self-control, one makes others suffer unjustly through punishment, imprisonment, destruction of wealth, character assassination, and banishment."[8]

We have only to look at some former world leaders—those who fell from grace—to see the truth of this statement. They destroyed nations, wiped out generations, and caused immeasurable suffering to humankind because they greedily sought power. Their decisions were proved to be wrong not only because their course of action consisted of huge blunders but also because they never found the happiness they were desperately looking for.

Moreover, unwholesome and unprofitable actions provoked by blind lust provide more evidence in favor of Buddha's emphasis that a decision motivated by greed reflects little wisdom. "Uncontrollable lust causes mental blindness, blurred vision, and depleted wisdom," observed Ananda. Consequently, one who is driven by lust "commits unwholesome actions through words, deeds, and thoughts." These actions cause "harmful effects on oneself, on others, and on both oneself and others."[9] The damaging consequences produced by lust-driven decisions confirm the absence of wisdom in such decisions.

Overall, Buddha clarified how greed, the uncurbed and unmanaged inner tendency for sensual pleasure and power, would drag people into unwise decisions. Blinded by their uncontrollable desire to please themselves and to raise their social standing, greedy people often tend to take falsehood as truth. Consequently, they make themselves unsuitable for rational decisions. The ineffectiveness and the impending harm of their actions attest to the absence of wisdom in their decisions.

How malice drains wisdom out of a decision

The term "malice," used for convenience, also represents a broad meaning. Buddha used such words as *dosa* (hatred, ill will), *kodha* (anger), *upanaha* (grudge, ill will, enmity), and *aghata* (hurtfulness) to explain this mental condition. All these words signify complex manifestations of a single human tendency: the urge and the effort to destroy any source of dissatisfaction and frustration. Buddha explained how a decision motivated by this destructive tendency would fail to reflect the decision maker's wisdom.

Buddha observed a close connection between greed and malice. Both tend to drain wisdom out of a decision in much the same way. When greed arises in the mind, malice also appears to further debilitate the individual's wise judgment. As Buddha explained, both greed and malice give rise to inner blindness that prevents people from differentiating between what is beneficial and what is not. Both provoke actions that lead people to unhappiness. Both greed and malice jointly hamper the wisdom of people's decisions.

Apart from this hand-in-hand process, malice also plays its own harmful part in human decisions in many ways. In particular, malicious thoughts tend to implant a profoundly false belief in the human mind, the belief that hate-oriented actions can solve problems and resolve conflicts. Driven by this false conviction, people in conflicts continue to sharpen their techniques to hurt the opposition. In doing so, they only make an already unpleasant situation worse.

"Hatred can never be conquered by hatred," proclaimed Buddha.[10] Citing a parable to clarify this utterance, he indicated how conflicts tend to gather momentum and cause increasing devastation as people rely on hate-oriented decisions to solve their conflicts.[11] As he explained, malice prevents people from seeing this truth and leads them to make decisions that would actually make problems worse rather than solve them. Therefore, malice takes wisdom away from a decision.

Buddha's attitude toward war further confirms his assertion that a decision impelled by malice only produces unwholesome effects and, therefore, contains no rationality.[12] The warriors of the Sakiya and Koliya kingdoms decided to fight against each other in order to solve a dispute over the use of water resources. Buddha intervened and urged the two clans to refrain from fighting. He made it clear that the problem could be solved not by fighting but by sharing the water resources so that both parties could feel satisfied. In other words, Buddha suggested that anger and revengeful thoughts, the immediate inner motives for fighting, would cause suffering for both sides. He implied that an anger-driven reaction would distract people from arriving at rational conclusions.

Buddha's poetic description of an angry person's mental and physical actions[13] is still the best example of how a decision made under the influence of ill will goes against the wisdom of the decision maker. Owing to its length, this beautiful and meaningful poem is not quoted here. Yet a summary will help us see how anger-driven decisions exhibit the decision maker's absurdity rather than his or her sagacity.

Throughout, the poem stressed that anger would suppress people's rational thinking, leading them to irrational behavior. Driven by anger, they use foul language and exhibit neither shame nor fear in committing unwholesome deeds. Sadly, anger makes them fall into dreadful blindness, urging them to destroy the lives of their own family members and other people alike. To make its blindness more complete, anger entices people to take their own lives, the dearest of all their possessions. In brief, anger negates wisdom in a decision because the indomitable strength of anger transforms a normal individual into a senseless rogue.

Obviously, malice—hatred, grudge-bearing, revengeful thoughts, anger, and so on—leads to a decision devoid of wisdom. Joined together with greed, it heightens its debilitating effects on human decisions. Malicious thoughts create the illusionary impression that problems can be solved through violence. Again, the same imbalanced state of mind baffles the decision maker, dragging the person to totally irrational conclusions. This confusing and misleading mental process clearly indicates how malice eliminates wisdom from a decision.

Right Evaluation 2: Absence of wrong motivations leads to right decisions

Buddha saw the absence of wrong motivations as essential in order to bring wisdom into decisions. The meaning of this view is twofold. First, before making a decision, we should make sure that our minds are not dominated by greed, malice, and illusion. Next, we should convince ourselves that the unwholesome motivations have been replaced by right thoughts. Since the "illusionary thought" has already drawn sufficient attention in the previous chapter, we will now clarify the connection between wise decisions and the absence of greed and malice.

How absence of greed leads to right decisions

We have already seen how greed tends to make a person's decision unwise. Being the voracious desire for self-gratification, greed blinds a person's vision and drives him or her to irrational and unwholesome conclusions. In contrast, the absence of greed brightens one's wisdom, paving the way for "numerous wholesome effects."[14]

As Buddha's disciple Ananda clarified, non-greed would establish mental calmness, safeguard individual morality, and enhance the ability to differentiate between beneficial and non-beneficial actions.[15] In this manner, the absence of greed in the mind prepares the background for an individual to make judicious decisions.

As various Suttas consistently emphasized, mental calmness is the foundation for wisdom. While greed breeds more desire, similar to an all-conquering king's hunger for more lands beyond the ocean,[16] subdued greed brings peace of mind. This mental condition is a clear indicator of one's ability to make rational decisions.

Notably, two characteristics in the greed-subdued mind contribute to the person's mental peace. First, inner suffering or an unsatisfactory state of mind, the companion of burning desire, no longer disturbs the person. Second, dejection and frustration, the harbingers of greed-related pleasure seeking, no longer continue to harrow the person. As a result, peacefulness settles in the mind, facilitating the person's ability to decide on the actions that are beneficial to himself or herself and to others.[17]

The following utterance of Buddha shows another aspect of improved wisdom in a greed-subdued mind. Controlled greed guides a person's social and political ascendancy in the most appropriate manner:

> Freed from greed, relieved from greed, and undisturbed by greed, a person who seeks power stops causing unjust suffering to others through punishment, imprisonment, destruction of wealth, abuse, or banishment.[18]

These crucial words convey an enlightening message. When greed submerges, respect for morality—a clear sign of wisdom—begins to shine within the individual. A person seeking power understands that causing harm to others is not the way to achieve his or her objectives.

The same utterance also shows how controlled greed appeals to the wisdom of political leaders. They understand that oppression and destruction would not be the appropriate actions to safeguard their power. They may still use punishment but not to cause undue pain in innocent people.

The ability to differentiate between beneficial and non-beneficial actions is the most noticeable skill that the absence of greed implants in the individual. To sum up, "greed gone, one sees what is beneficial to oneself, what is beneficial to others, and what is beneficial to both parties."[19]

How absence of malicious thoughts makes a decision wise

As previously discussed, Buddha observed that both greed and hatred connect to influence human decisions in a negative way. Together, they rigorously suppress human rationality, thus inhibiting the wisdom in one's actions. The submergence of the two negative motivations, in contrast, jointly contributes to wise decisions.

On numerous occasions, Buddha explained how it works. Similar to what non-greed does, the absence of hatred also brings about mental clarity and implants morality in the mind. This frame of mind improves the individual's ability to make the most appropriate decisions. As already mentioned, greed and malice, according to Buddha's definition, are the two most dominant negative forces in the human mind. They darken the vision and impair the judgment. As both forces lose their grip on the mind, people regain their vision, and their rational thinking is restored.

From Buddha's viewpoint, eradication of malicious thoughts, in fact, is the individual's highest achievement. Untainted by malice, the most harmful motivation, a decision should show more rationality, more wisdom. The phrase "absence of malicious thoughts" does not suggest the necessity of having a blank mind at the time one makes a decision. Rather, this phrase means the presence of compassion and respect as a requirement for a right decision. The absence of ill will (e.g., anger, hatred, revengefulness) does not leave the mind empty; rather, it allows love and compassion to pour in. Therefore, when malicious thoughts depart, loving-kindness takes their place to help evaluate the forthcoming decision.

This change is the turning point to enhance the wisdom of a decision. We previously discussed how a person, when overwhelmed by both greed and malice, fails to evaluate the effectiveness of a decision.

Basically, greedy and malicious thoughts depict a false picture about the benefits and harmful effects of one's decision. Now the strength of greed and malice has diminished, and a new scale has replaced it. Subsequently, a decision maker tends to display a vastly improved ability to make better decisions.

How does loving-kindness provide such a strong support for correct decisions? To answer this question, we first need to focus on the meaning of the term "loving-kindness." To repeat a previous remark, translations of the original Pali words are not perfect, and "loving-kindness" may convey the idea that one should ignore one's own well-being and pay overwhelming attention to others' welfare as a criterion for rational decisions.

However, Buddha's advice is that one should never concede one's own well-being to that of others. In other words, love and respect for oneself represent an essential part of loving-kindness. The rise of these feelings during the process of decision making signifies a balanced and respectful evaluation of the benefits that a decision would offer to oneself and to others involved in the decision.

So, the people who pave the way for loving-kindness acquire the ability to develop a balanced reasoning regarding decisions. Mindful of their own progress and compassionate toward others, they understand that their decisions should bring wholesome effects for both parties. Absence of malicious thoughts and the presence of loving-kindness thus enhance the decision maker's wisdom.

Right Evaluation 3: Consequences of a decision make it right or wrong

Buddha consistently emphasized that, for a decision to be right, it should also be evaluated in terms of its possible consequences. The most notable point in this emphasis is that correct motivation alone would not make a decision completely right. Besides ensuring the presence of wholesome motivations, the decision maker should also consider the possible consequences of the decision.

Of course, reduced greed and ill will and cultivated loving-kindness lay the foundation for wise judgment. Still, Buddha stressed that one should learn how to construct a rational argumentation upon that foundation in order to reach a rational conclusion.

To clarify this point, let us look at the following comments of a young female college student who gave a ride to two male students after a drunken party:

> It was a big bash, and we all sang and danced into the night. The guys were drunk, and I didn't want them to crash or get caught by a cop while going back to the dorm. I had talked to them at school, and they were very decent boys. So I thought I should give them a ride.

Obviously, the decision seems to have been motivated by right feelings: she did not want the two boys to get into trouble. However, one may question the extent to which she used her wisdom when she offered a ride to two drunken boys at night. The police officer who investigated the sexual assault that happened on the way back to the dorm had the answer: "She helped the wrong people at the wrong time." Even though the female student was motivated by compassion, her decision failed to reflect wise judgment because she did not evaluate the possible consequences of her decision.

How a decision should be evaluated in terms of its consequences

Several Suttas have explained what Buddha meant by the term "evaluation of an action according to the consequences." To complete this evaluation successfully, first we need to answer the following three questions carefully:

1. Does the decision lead to my own well-being (*atta samhita*)?
2. Does the decision lead to the well-being of others who

are involved in the decision (*parattha samhita*)?
3. Does the decision lead to the well-being of both myself and others involved (*ubhayattha samhita*)?[20]

We previously discussed Buddha's assertion that one should never disregard one's own well-being for any reason. By urging his listeners to make decisions that would lead to their well-being, Buddha explained how one should care about one's own success and happiness. Still, a lopsided decision that leads only to the decision maker's well-being is not acceptable, either. Buddha's view is that a decision should provide welfare not only for the decision maker but also for those affected by the decision.

Kalama Sutta indicated that the word "well-being" (*samhita*) contains a broad meaning. Three Pali words—*atthaya, hitaya*, and *sukhaya*—defined the word "well-being." *Atthaya* and *hitaya* refer to the benefits that a decision brings to both the decision maker and others. *Sukhaya* indicates happiness associated with a decision. The two words "benefit" and "happiness" seem difficult to separate. Yet, obviously, Buddha used two different words because he noticed a difference between benefit and happiness.

We observe that a beneficial decision may not always cause happiness. Similarly, a decision that would bring immediate happiness may not be beneficial at all. What is important is to have a balanced evaluation of both the benefits and the happiness that a decision would bring to the decision maker.

Besides, the evaluation of a decision in terms of its consequences would never be complete if the decision maker were to ignore the people who would be affected by the decision. Most decisions people make do have an effect on others, and the decision maker should be aware that his or her decision must not affect others adversely. In other words, even though Buddha defended self-benefit as a positive effect of a decision, he never admitted it to be the sole criterion. A given decision, of course, would bring benefits to the decision maker. However, if the same decision causes misery to others, the person should, essentially, refrain from making that decision.

The usefulness of this evaluation seems invaluable in modern society. Today, a few people are usually entrusted to make decisions that can influence a great majority. Political and business decisions, in particular, appear to merit this evaluation.

Driven by self-promotion (greed) and ill will, some leaders may prefer violence. They ignore the enormous suffering such a decision would bring upon the public. Urged by the sole motivation of making profits, business people cheat society. They too disregard the happiness and well-being of the public. From Buddha's point of view, both approaches have failed to go through a right evaluation because they depend on mere self-interest and ignore the benefit and happiness of others.

As Buddha stressed, only with a balanced evaluation of a decision's effects on oneself and others can one reach a rational conclusion. The extreme forms of both selfishness and selflessness hinder wise judgment. Moderation, in contrast, paves the way for wisdom.

Right Evaluation 4: Attention to the views of qualified people leads to right decisions

Buddha also explained that approval by the wise (*vinnupasattha*) and rejection by the wise (*vinnugarahita*) are dependable reasons for a person to judge the wisdom of a decision.[21] This statement means that a decision might be correct or incorrect, depending on whether qualified people approve or reject the same decision. Buddha insisted that we should apply this criterion when we decide to abandon something or to "accept and live accordingly."

The important question is, "Who is the qualified person?" The Pali word for "the qualified person" is *vinnu*. Interestingly, both *vinnu* and "know" derive from the same Sanskrit root *jhana*, which means "knowledge," "wisdom," or "education." A *vinnu* is translated as "the person who is intelligent, wise, or learned." In brief, those who possess the ability to reason wisely and to manage greed and malice are the wise people. Those who have expert knowledge in a certain field are the learned people. Buddha's emphasis is that the opinions of such people can be trusted when a person wants a rational conclusion.

In this sense the following argument is correct:

> I should quit smoking because my doctor told me that I might develop heart problems as a result of my smoking.

The decision to quit smoking is a wise judgment because that decision was encouraged by learned persons in that particular field. Importantly, however, if the learned person lacks wisdom, attention to that person's opinion can lead an individual into unwise decisions. A qualified person to depend on for decisions is one who possesses both knowledge and wisdom.

Summary

Overall, Buddha, having rejected fallacious argumentation, offered us freedom to rationally evaluate a decision. Essentially, the evaluation of both the intention and the possible consequences of a decision paves the way for us to arrive at the most rational decisions. Attention to the views of qualified people also facilitates making the right decision. The same decision should be evaluated from all points of view in order to make its rationality complete.

The phrase "humanistic pragmatism," which suggests the practical usefulness of a decision to everybody involved, sums up Buddha's values in decision making. We should consider both self-benefits and others' well-being while evaluating the effectiveness of a decision. After all, *I* (any person) deserves the right to make the ultimate decision, but *I* also must take the responsibility for the consequences of that decision.

Chapter Twelve

····································

The Eight Most Important Don't-do Habits for Daily Practice

Disciplined actions and disciplined

words are a blessing to the layperson.

Buddha, the *Sutta Nipata*

As discussed in the last two chapters, Buddha introduced a complete set of criteria for his followers to evaluate their decisions. In addition, using the same criteria, he also presented a list of actions that individuals should refrain from doing. He selected mostly the natural human urges that appeared to him as wrongful, and persuaded people not to be driven by these tendencies. This chapter will detail the actions Buddha wanted his followers to give up as being wrongful deeds.

Five of these habits are generally categorized as the Five Precepts. Some believe that the Five Precepts are simple, strict, and clear-cut rules. However, a close observation of Buddha's relevant speeches reveals that this belief is not always correct. The Five Precepts, in fact, are different from how they appear: the Pali words in each precept do not present a clear view of it. As we go on with this discussion, we will clarify what Buddha actually meant by the Five Precepts, but first let us take each of the eight rules separately for an orderly discussion.

1. Do not destroy life

Destruction of life is the first action Buddha always asked his lay followers to refrain from. To understand this practice correctly, we first need to study the Pali term Buddha used to convey this idea. He said *panatipata veramani* or *panatipata pativirato* to convey this advice. The words *veramani* and *pativirato* may be translated as "refraining from." However, *panatipata* is a compound word: *pana* (a living being)+*ati* (upon or toward)+*pata* (fall). This word can hardly be translated by a single English word. Precisely, it means attacking a human being, or any living being, either with a weapon or physical force. Killing of both humans and animals is included in the first of the Five Precepts.

This advice found a preeminent position in Buddha's teaching because he promoted great respect for life. To Buddha, any form of life, especially human and animal life, were worthy of respect. Of course, life should depend on life for existence, but Buddha never tolerated wanton destruction of life.

What kinds of killing are included in this precept?

A close study of the *Sutta Pitaka* reveals that "destruction of life" includes the following forms of killing:

A. Homicide

Unarguably, homicide is an act of destroying life, according to Buddha. He never allowed individuals or groups to kill other humans. "In the same way I protect my life, others also value their lives, shun death, and look for happiness," Buddha explained. "Then how can one kill another?"[1] With this attitude, Buddha always persuaded his community to respect fellow humans, and not to take their lives.

Buddha's unequivocal rejection of homicide was based on several factors. First, he valued human life more than anything else. "To be born as a human being is a rare opportunity," he stated.[2] Human life is so precious in Buddha's teaching because only a human being can attain Nibbana, the highest level of inner development. Next, Buddha's philosophy never tolerated the fear and pain caused by killing. Considering these two factors, Buddha clearly proclaimed that homicide would mean destruction of life.

B. Suicide

Taking one's own life, according to Buddha, is another manifestation of destroying life. He did not believe that suicide is a solution to human problems. What he emphasized throughout his speeches was the fruitfulness of human effort. Being an embodiment of great potential, a human being should learn not to run away from problems, but to challenge them. Killing oneself is an act of denying the enormous potential with which a human being is naturally endowed.

Buddha was one of the first to stand against suicide. More importantly, he may be the first ever to prevent a suicide through counseling. When the teenage girl Rajjumala, who worked as a housemaid, tried to take her life, Buddha volunteered to help her. She told Buddha that she had lost interest in life because her employer continued to mistreat her. Buddha comforted the child and talked to the lady who employed her. He found that the child had been treated as a slave. Buddha eventually persuaded the lady to adopt Rajjumala as her own daughter.[3] This remarkable story highlights not only Buddha's loving concern toward human problems but also his opposition to suicide.

Buddha identified suicidal tendencies as an imbalanced state of mind. He said, "Driven by illusion (*mucchita*), people cut themselves with swords, take poison, hang themselves, and throw themselves from rocks."[4] This utterance further clarifies his position regarding suicide. Wise judgment is absent in a person who attempts to take his or her life. In the presence of inner disturbances, one should strive to gain wisdom, rather than take one's life.

Exceptions

Two examples in the *Sutta Pitaka,* however, stand out as unique exceptions.[5] Buddha found no fault with two of his ordained disciples who committed suicide after developing incurable diseases and suffering from intense pain. These examples may open peripheral topics, but what is obvious is that Buddha never encouraged suicide as a solution to human conflicts and inner problems. Killing oneself to escape problems is an act of destroying life.

C. Killing animals as a source of enjoyment

Killing as a source of enjoyment can be categorized as destruction of life, according to Buddha's viewpoint. Compassionate Buddha never encouraged humans to express joy at the sight of a suffering animal. One day, on his way to the city of Savatthi, Buddha saw a group of young children attacking a snake. He found that the motive behind the children's attack was to seek cruel pleasure by watching the snake suffer. Buddha helped the children understand the cruelty of their act.

He made his point clear by saying, "Those who harm animals as a source of enjoyment would never find happiness."[6] Buddha clearly rejected the killing of animals as a source of joy and amusement.

D. Animal sacrifice

Animal sacrifice, according to Buddha, belongs in the same category as destroying life. Killing animals to please deities was a prevalent practice during Buddha's time. In these sacrifices, animals were tied and even hung during the long period of prayer before they were killed. Several Suttas indicate that Buddha vehemently objected to such sacrifices.

In *Kutadanta Sutta*,[7] Buddha cited a parable to emphasize the uselessness and cruelty of animal sacrifices. He noted that the ancient king Mahavijita made a great sacrifice to deities without animal bloodshed. "In that sacrifice, not a single ox, goat, fowl, or pig was slain," Buddha noted. "With ghee, oil, butter, milk, honey, and sugar," the great king was able to acquire the perfect blessing of the deities. Even the attendants to the harmless sacrifice of King Mahavijita "carried on their work without tears on their faces" since no animals were killed.

Buddha made it clear that animal sacrifice is a huge waste, as well as an instance of human cruelty. Addressing believers in animal sacrifice, Buddha asserted that they would obtain the perfect blessing from deities without bloodshed.

What about killing for food?

One of the perennial arguments regarding human ethics is whether killing is acceptable as a means of obtaining food. A great majority of people still believe that animals should be killed and eaten. However, a steadily increasing number of people assert that animals should not be a source of food for humans. We will find Buddha's position on this controversial topic interesting and useful.

Buddha's opinion about eating animal flesh was clearly dependent on other relevant factors. His permission for Bhikkhus to accept meat and fish if the animals were not specially killed for them bears witness to his position. Importantly, Bhikkhus never prepared their own meals. They carried a bowl and walked from house to house once a day for alms. They had to accept what was given to them, which was almost always a portion of what the people had prepared for themselves.

With wildlife so abundant and human population so sparse, people in that society ate mostly meat. Bhikkhus had no choice but to eat what they received from people. This example suggests that human beings may depend on animal life for sustenance when no choice is available other than eating animal flesh.

An important Sutta in the *Anguttara Nikaya* confirms Buddha's position. In this Sutta he advised lay followers to avoid dependence on animal flesh if they had physical strength (*viriya*).[8] Almost certainly, this utterance indicates that one who has enough physical strength to work should engage in agriculture rather than use easy methods of killing domesticated animals or trapping wild beasts for food.

In other words, a sick, helpless person may set a snare to catch a wild animal but, after regaining strength, that person should cultivate land. Under normal conditions, using animals as a source of food would be wrong, but in a desperate situation the individual decision could be otherwise.

Buddha cited an individual's lack of physical strength as an acceptable reason to live on animal flesh because that situation was obvious in his society. In other societies and situations, however, different causes would force people to survive on animal flesh. People living close to the North Pole, for instance, would hardly find any agricultural products to eat. As a result, they, inevitably, have to kill and eat animals in order to survive. Buddha's words indicate that people who encounter such unusual difficulties in finding agricultural products may survive on animal flesh rather than starve.

Nevertheless, Buddha's teaching strongly suggests that people may not kill animals for food or buy animal flesh when other food is abundant. Greed for animal flesh, particularly when sufficient, nutritious food is obtainable through harmless methods, indicates encouragement of killing, according to Buddha's ethics.

2. Do not take anything wrongfully

The next don't-do habit, as it occurs in the Five Precepts, is *adinna+adana veramani*, literally, "keeping away from seizing what is not given." This precept is generally defined as abstaining from stealing, but the Pali term certainly covers a broader meaning than this conventional definition.

The phrase *adinna+adana* includes bribery, burglary, forceful acquisition of property, invasion of somebody else's territory, fraud, theft, or any other deceitful way of obtaining money, material objects, or other benefits.

Buddha observed numerous forms of "taking what is not given" that were prevalent in his society. A household servant would steal money or other objects from the house in which he or she was employed. A housewife would cheat her husband over the family wealth he had entrusted to her. Organized thieves would plunder towns and villages. A merchant would cheat a customer, a group of robbers would ambush travelers, and one who sought great fortune would take bribes. Obviously, all these different manifestations of wrongful acquisition, which occur in various Suttas, are included in this don't-do advice.

The key phrase that defines this wrongful practice is "taking by means of theft or stealing what is not given."[9] Clearly, this definition conveys a broader meaning than what is generally accepted as stealing. Buddha obviously urged his followers to refrain from taking any deceitful, corruptive, or forceful steps as a means to obtaining material success.

3. Avoid misconduct in sensory satisfaction

The next daily observance Buddha recommended to his lay followers was to avoid misconduct in sensory pleasure (*kamesu micchacara veramani*). *Kamesu* means "in any form of sensory satisfaction." *Micchacara* is a compound word that means "wrong conduct." This advice is meant to guide people's sensory satisfaction in such a way that their search for sensual pleasure should not be a burden to themselves and others.

Even though "misconduct" refers to any form of sensory satisfaction, it specifically focuses on human sexuality. As previously mentioned, Buddha recognized sexuality as a powerful human urge. He remarked that both men and women would find no better sight, sound, smell, or touch than that of the opposite sex.[10] The human urge for physical satisfaction being so predominant, Buddha offered extra assistance for his lay followers to manage their desire.

What sexual behavior represents misconduct?

Even though Buddha did not categorize all forms of sexual misconduct in a single speech, close attention to his speeches helps us to identify the acts that he classified as sexual misconduct. We will briefly discuss each of these acts that he persuaded society to refrain from.

A. Unfaithfulness in a committed relationship

A committed relationship, as Buddha recognized in *Sigalovada Sutta*, is one in which both partners would fulfill their duties and responsibilities toward each other. Buddha suggested that both the male and the female in such a relationship should abstain from seeking other relationships.

However, the proposed faithfulness to each other seems conditional. A man or a woman is not destined to remain committed to his or her partner forever simply because he or she began a relationship with the other. One partner's irresponsibility and negligence of his or her own duty and obligation, including faithfulness, would allow the other partner to leave and seek a different relationship.

The following words of Buddha shed light on this idea:

> A wife should not disregard [*na atimannati*] a husband who displays enthusiasm, strives [for success], provides for the needs of his wife, and always takes care of her.[11]

This statement hints that commitment should be mutual. In Buddha's society, men were responsible for accumulating wealth. Buddha suggested that they had to be active and strive for success. They also had to use the wealth in order to take care of their wives and to provide comfort for them. A wife should not disregard such a dutiful husband.

The same quotation also implies a wife's rights to disregard a husband who habitually exhibits no interest in success, wastes his time, and neglects his duties toward her. *Atimannati*, the Pali word quoted above, has multiple meanings, such as "neglect," "disregard," and "despise." A wife might be free to find another life partner in case her husband blatantly ignores his duties toward her and the family.

Of course, Buddha did not suggest that one might seek extramarital relationships when one's partner fails to be dutiful. Instead, he apparently meant that finding a dutiful partner would be better than remaining faithful to a person who would neglect his or her duties. Buddha offered both men and women the freedom to leave uncommitted partners and to choose better persons.

Still, Buddha maintained that, when one partner is dutiful and faithful, the other partner should also remain committed to the relationship. A person's involvement with others while being in a committed relationship means sexual misconduct, according to Buddha.

B. Seduction

Also, Buddha specified that seduction—solicitation of sex through lies, false promises, and irrational appeals—should be categorized as sexual misconduct. In *Veludvareyya Sutta* Buddha asked his lay community members to refrain from seduction as a part of their effort to avoid sexual misconduct. He asked men to compare their feelings to others' in the following manner: "I detest others who seduce my wife. In the same way, others would dislike my own seduction of their wives."[12] Buddha explained that this comparison would facilitate their understanding of seduction as sexual misconduct.

C. Forced sex

This form of sexual misconduct includes any sexual assault, such as uninvited sexual advances, harassment, and rape. Buddha never permitted violence. Harmlessness should predominate over all human actions. Forced sex violates this most important principle; therefore, sexual assault is unacceptable, according to Buddha's philosophy.

Buddha identified abstinence from forced sex as a sign of worldly progress for laypeople.[13] In his examples, Buddha pointed at men as those who would commit such wrongful deeds. They would approach single or married women who are under the protection of others,[14] or force their victims to participate in sexual acts.[15] Buddha advised men to abstain from such wrong deeds. Overall, he considered any forceful sexual behavior as sexual misconduct.

D. Incest

Buddha also rejected incest as sexual misconduct. He did not tolerate incest even if such a sexual relationship was based on mutual consent.[16] Buddha observed that abstaining from incest is a social rule, but he respected it for its benefits. He identified incest as a sign of human degeneration.[17] This observation indicates that Buddha urged his lay community to stay away from incest because doing so would contribute to both individual and social progress.

E. Sexual abuse of minors

Buddha considered sexual abuse of minors as another form of sexual misconduct. This idea is evident in Buddha's remarks that those who abuse sexually immature people are lower than dogs.[18] To emphasize the baseness of child abusers, Buddha mentioned that even male dogs would not mate with sexually immature females. Anybody who sexually abuses children violates an ethical code that even dogs respect. Buddha's intense dislike for child abuse indicates that he clearly regarded the sexual abuse of minors as a form of sexual misconduct.

F. Overindulgence in sex

The other form of sexual misconduct, as Buddha saw it, was overindulgence in sex. For the layperson, Buddha always emphasized moderation in all forms of sensory satisfaction. Self-indulgence is at one extreme; self-denial is at the other. Moderation means avoidance of both extremes. This middle path is clearly applicable to the layperson's enjoyment of sexual pleasures as well. Buddha's phrase "right measure," which he specifically used to indicate moderate eating, can be extended to all forms of sensory satisfaction, including the satisfaction of sexual desires.

In a general sense, the phrase "overindulgence in sex" defies a simple definition. It can be engagement in multiple sexual relationships, overemphasis of sex with a single partner, or a keen search for different methods of sexual satisfaction. One's attitude toward sex seems to set the boundaries for moderation and indulgence. The erroneous view that constant gratification of sexual desires leads a person to happiness seems to be the attitude that takes a person beyond moderation.

Apparently, Buddha did not maintain that reproduction is the only purpose of a romantic relationship between a man and a woman. Instead, he regarded such a relationship as a source of joy for a layperson. Buddha's utterance "One should be happy (*santuttho*) with one's own wife, without seeking other women"[19] conveys this idea. The word "*santuttho*" includes a sexual connotation. The urge for sex is not something to suppress consistently. Instead, it is something for a layperson to express. However, he or she should be aware of the limits that define moderation.

What about premarital sex and homosexuality?

The six forms of sexual conduct discussed above seem to cover everything about sexual misbehavior as it was defined by Buddha. We find no information about premarital sex and homosexuality in his speeches. The most appropriate approach is to evaluate both practices in terms of general criteria of good and bad as recommended by Buddha. As previously discussed, unwholesome intention behind an action and the negative effects resulting from an action are the main criteria to be considered in evaluating an action. We need to use the same criteria to determine whether premarital sex and same-sex relationships are acceptable.

Considering its adverse effects, we may conclude that premarital sex during the teenage years in particular would run counter to Buddha's teaching. This conclusion is based on young adults' vulnerability to unwanted parenthood, sexually transmitted diseases, and a host of other disadvantages.

With regard to same-sex relationships, we find it difficult to come to a clear conclusion. However, one of the greatest concepts in Buddha's teaching was individual freedom of choice. A harmless substitution for the traditional male-female sexual relationship does not seem to contradict Buddha's criteria of evaluating an action.

4. Do not speak untruths with wrong intention

Buddha advised his lay community to refrain from speaking untruths that have their roots in the wrong intention. The phrase "wrong intention" is a key term in this precept. We need to examine our own thoughts to find out the motive behind speaking an untruth. If the motive is to gain unfair advantage or to cause any harm, that untruth is a lie.

The Pali term Buddha constantly used to mean avoidance of telling lies was *musavada veramani.* This term is often translated as "refraining from telling lies," but this translation seems inadequate and even misleading. We need to know the connotative meaning of the word *musavada* to understand what Buddha actually meant by this precept.

Even though the word *musavada* occurs hundreds of times in the *Sutta Pitaka,* the explanation of the term, similar to that of many others, is always brief. Nevertheless, certain passages in the Suttas offer some clues as to what Buddha meant by *musavada.* The following quotation is just one example:

> If someone destroys my welfare with lies, that act is unpleasant to me. If I do the same, my own act would be unpleasant to others . . . One who reflects thus should refrain from *musavada.*[20]

This quotation indicates that false speech is characterized by the speaker's intention to cause destruction of others' welfare. Unwholesome intention and the impending harmful effects are the decisive factors of false speech. Various Suttas indicate that many kinds of false speech cause harm and, therefore, should be avoided. We will briefly refer to some of these categories.

A. False report

False report is one obvious form of lying that Buddha asked his followers to refrain from. In Buddha's society, numerous thinkers were ardently campaigning for followers. Some supporters of different schools of thought intentionally distorted a speech given by an opposing leader in a sinister plan to harm the reputation of such a leader. On several occasions, Buddha found his own speeches being intentionally misinterpreted to harm his reputation. He called such distortion a harmful act that should be avoided.

B. False accusation and perjury

False accusation and perjury are two more manifestations of lying that Buddha wanted his listeners to avoid. *Mahasihanada Sutta*[21] provided an example of false accusation that Buddha disapproved of. He remarked that in a public or private dealing with somebody else's wrongdoing, one should speak about "only what had happened."[22] He identified perjury as a practice that would cause harm to the speaker, as well as to others. Both practices are lies that people should do away with.

C. False promise

Making false promises to gain advantage is another form of lying that Buddha regarded as harmful, and requested his followers to abstain from. He recognized those who provide mere lip service as liars of that sort.[23] One who might give various excuses to avoid one's duty to a friend despite one's ability to fulfill such a duty would also belong to the same category of liars.[24] Some others might "deceive a Brahmin, an ordained person, or any clergyman by telling lies."[25] The deception in this case would be the intention of the pupil to learn from the holy person after giving false promises about fulfilling his or her duty. In all these cases, the ulterior motive of deception is the sign that characterizes a speech as false.

D. False self-presentation

Buddha remarked that false self-presentation is another form of lying from which his followers should refrain. This false speech includes giving false information about one's qualifications, skills, achievements, and conduct in order to gain undeserved advantages.

As Buddha observed, exaggeration of one's spiritual qualifications would be an example of false self-presentation. Some spiritual teachers in Buddha's society strove to win popularity and gain disciples by making false claims about their spiritual achievements. Buddha asked his disciples never to make such false claims. One's effort to hide one's own wrongdoings and to present oneself as a virtuous person also belongs to false self-presentation. Buddha remarked that inadequate personality development would be a reason for such behavior.

Speaking untruth as a means to a wholesome purpose

Speaking untruth, from Buddha's viewpoint, would be acceptable as long as such an act follows a wholesome intention and serves a wholesome purpose. In fact, the word "lie" would be inappropriate to mean a false statement thus made. Buddha himself used both "apparent" and "actual" untruth as a rhetorical technique to guide people toward wholesome decisions and actions.

For instance, Kesi, a horse trainer, told Buddha that he (Kesi) would kill the horses that were untamable. Buddha immediately replied that he (Buddha) would also "kill" the people who would never succeed in achieving inner progress. Stunned by Buddha's reply, Kesi retorted that he wondered how Buddha, who taught loving-kindness, would kill people. Buddha then said that his use of the word "killing" meant "leaving out."[26] In other words, he made an apparently untrue statement to convince his listener that sending the untamable horses back to the jungle would be a better choice than killing them.

Moreover, Buddha made statements that were actually untrue to help his listeners in various situations. Silence, of course, was one technique he used to postpone speaking the truth. However, evidence clearly supports instances when he intentionally presented untruth as another means to wait for the right time to speak the truth.

One clear example is Buddha's assurance to Gotami that her dead child's life could be restored. For the baby's treatment, he asked Gotami to bring a handful of mustard seeds from a family in which no death had taken place. Buddha observed that telling the truth (that the dead child's life could not be restored) would be harmful to Gotami since she was so distraught at the time. With that awareness, Buddha used actual untruth as a means to put off telling the truth. That approach led Gotami to accept her child's death calmly.

These examples and many others found in the *Sutta Pitaka* suggest that Buddha demonstrated the use of untruth as a useful practice to help his listeners. Evidently, his interpretation of lying clearly meets the criteria of good and bad he generally recommended for his followers. An utterance or a rhetorical expression may not be regarded as a lie simply because it contains a deliberately expressed untruth. Unwholesome intention is the key factor that would determine an expression to be a lie.

5. Do not allow alcohol to cause physical and mental imbalance

The last of the Five Precepts, this don't-do habit has given rise to much controversy. Some argue that this precept means total abstinence from all kinds of intoxicants. Others believe that it means controlled use of alcohol. Let us examine this precept closely to find out its most probable meaning.

The Pali term for this controversial precept is *suramerayamajja-pamadatthana veramani.* "Abstaining from" is the meaning of *veramani*, but the first word of this precept is tricky and ambiguous. It is a compound term with five words joined together. *Sura, meraya,* and *majja* seemingly refer to three kinds of intoxicating drinks that people used during Buddha's time. *Pamada,* a technical Pali word meaning "heedlessness," "inattention," or "delay," suggests the drinker's inability to do the right act or to make the right decision. *Thana* has several meanings, but in this precept it means "able to cause." The entire precept thus means "abstention from intoxication that would cause mental imbalance and physical torpidity."

A subtle ambiguity lies hidden in the translation, as well as in the original precept. Did Buddha urge his lay community to refrain from the very practice of drinking alcohol, which would generally cause mental imbalance and physical torpidity? If not, did he want them to refrain only from excessive use of alcohol, also a practice that would cause those same effects? In other words, did Buddha regard the given dangers as inherent to liquor itself, or to the excessive intake of liquor?

Buddha never imposed strict rules for his community members. Some traditions during Buddha's time held that alcohol was a divine drink, others that alcohol was essential for happiness and health. Given this social background, we find it difficult to believe that Buddha strongly persuaded his lay followers to do away with alcohol completely. In his advice to Sigala, Buddha mentioned that one should not indulge in alcohol because such indulgence would cause one to get sick and to lose wealth.[27] Buddha was more concerned about the effect on his lay followers' mental and physical behavior, and the loss of wealth caused by alcohol.

Apparently, Buddha recommended this precept to prevent his lay followers' excessive and habitual use of alcohol, or, in other words, alcohol abuse. All evidence considered, Pali scholars Rhys Davids' and William Stede's translation of the precept in the *Pali-English Diction-ary*—"abstaining from any state of indolence arising from the use of intoxicants" (712)—seems more acceptable.

Drug abuse

We find no information in the Suttas about drug abuse because such a practice was not present in Buddha's society. Nevertheless, as it is practiced today, drug abuse is similar to alcohol abuse, and Buddha would have unequivocally asked his lay disciples to refrain from it.

Interestingly, the word "abuse" indicates the violation of one of Buddha's most important rules for lay life, the rule of avoiding extremes. Using drugs for medical purposes is the right way to use them. Taking drugs for illusionary sensory satisfaction is an instance of exceeding the limits of proper use. Thus, drug abuse clearly contradicts Buddha's basic philosophy for lay life.

Misuse of drugs also goes against Buddha's general criteria of evaluating an action. We have previously discussed how intentions behind an action, and also its consequences, jointly decide its effectiveness or invalidity. In drug abuse, we find neither wholesome intention nor wholesome effects. This evaluation clearly categorizes drug abuse as a degrading habit.

6. Do not use words to divide people

Avoidance of words that divide people is the next don't-do habit Buddha promoted among his followers. The Pali term for the word that causes division is *pisunavaca*. *Pisuna* means "malicious, slanderous, spiteful." *Vaca* suggests speech. Together, *pisunavaca* means "the use of language to split relationships." Buddha advised his listeners to keep away from such language.

Telling lies may also cause division among people, but a lie and a *pisunavaca* are different. Notably, a *pisunavaca* is a true or slightly exaggerated statement aimed at damaging a relationship. Buddha explained that "telling there what one heard here" and "telling here what one heard there" characterize the speech that would cause division among people.[28]

Buddha identified himself as a "promoter of unity through words."[29] Similarly, he instructed his disciples to "be fond of unity, to promote unity, and to use words to cause unity."[30] He insisted that his followers should avoid any form of speech that would threaten unity among people.

7. Refrain from using harsh language

In Chapter Eight, we referred to this habit as a prerequisite for healthy relationships. Avoiding harsh language is so important that Buddha advised his lay community to always be careful about how they spoke.

According to *Veludvareyya Sutta*, Buddha's lay followers should avoid harsh language because such language would be "unpleasant and unfriendly to the listener."[31] Soft words, in contrast, are "pleasing to the ear and go straight to the hearts of all."[32] Buddha strongly believed that verbal abuse would never help people to improve their behavior or to establish healthy relationships. Therefore, he cited avoidance of harsh language as one of the essential daily observances.

8. Avoid senseless talk

Finally, Buddha urged his listeners to practice "avoidance of senseless talk" as a daily habit. The phrase "senseless talk" covers a broad meaning. Its original Pali word is *samphappalapa*. Even though we have translated this Pali word as "senseless talk," we need to discuss Buddha's explanation of *samphappalapa* to understand its complete meaning.

Buddha identified six kinds of speech as belonging to senseless talk.[33] He advised his listeners to be mindful that their words would not belong to those categories. We will briefly discuss how speech becomes a *samphappalapa* or meaningless talk.

A. Words spoken at the wrong time

An expression inappropriate to the occasion is an example of senseless speech, according to Buddha's explanation. We previously discussed how Buddha identified himself as one who spoke at the right time. He explained that, to make a speech, conversation, or comment meaningful, the speaker should say it at the right time (*kalavadi*).

B. Words that contain untruth or exaggeration

Words that present false information as true belong to the category of senseless speech. Also included in this category are exaggeration and fabrication of news, events, occurrences, consequences, and accusations. Buddha's advice is that one should present true information (*bhutavadi*) in order to convince the listener.

C. Words that bring no benefit

Words that bring no benefit to the speaker or to the listener also belong to the group of senseless words. Self-display through words, long-winded conversations about others, and discussion of meaningless topics are some of the examples of unprofitable speech. We may be engaged in such conversations for hours but find no meaning in them. The opposite is the use of profitable words, or *atthavadi*, as Buddha called it.

D. Words that lead the listener to unwholesome thoughts and conduct

Buddha further indicated that words persuading the listener to unwholesome thoughts and actions also belong to *samphappalapa*. Mainly, manipulative language fits into this group. Such language may corrupt the listener's mind and appeal to his or her negative emotions. Overwhelmed by the power of such words, the listener would develop greed and ill will and commit harmful deeds. Buddha advised that words should encourage people toward wholesome thoughts and actions (*dhammavadi*) instead of leading them in the opposite direction.

E. Words that threaten the listener's self-discipline

Similar to words used for unwholesome persuasion are words that lead to the breakdown of self-discipline. Here, Buddha drew attention to the danger of using language as a means to lead the listener toward undisciplined actions. Words that persuade people to break rules and develop harmful habits may be included in this category of senseless words. The opposite of this practice is the use of words to promote the listener's self-discipline (*vinayavadi*).

F. Words that express trite and shallow ideas

Finally, when words express ideas that lack originality, novelty, and depth, such words also belong to the category of senseless speech. They are senseless because they neither demonstrate the speaker's wisdom nor benefit the listener. Buddha mentioned that words should express important views and ideas (*nidhanavati vaca*). Such words do not belong to the category of senseless speech.

According to Buddha, any verbal expression that fits any of these six descriptions is a *samphappalapa*, or senseless speech. Such expressions are both useless and harmful. Buddha advised his lay followers to reflect upon their speech before they spoke. Such an effort would prevent their words from falling into any of these categories.

Summary

The eight don't-do habits discussed in this chapter are the most important daily practices for the layperson. Even though the last three habits discussed above are not included in the Five Precepts, Buddha frequently emphasized the importance of their daily practice for the lay community. He prescribed these habits because they would enable his lay followers to develop their external behavior—physical and verbal actions—to the best of their capabilities. That individual development, in turn, would contribute to the progress of society.

Chapter Thirteen

....

How to Develop an Attractive Personality

Actions (words, deeds, and thoughts)
determine whether a person is well de-
veloped or not. Wisdom illuminates
his or her character.

Buddha, the *Gradual Sayings*

Personality development is not merely a peripheral topic but a focal point in Buddha's teaching. He mentioned that a main objective of our life should be to develop our personalities to the highest level. To enable his followers to achieve this objective, Buddha discussed various aspects related to personality development. He identified the characteristics that differentiate properly developed personalities from those that are inadequately developed. He examined why some people continue to improve slowly while others achieve a fast and thorough improvement. Above all, he revealed to his disciples the techniques that would allow them to construct attractive personalities. This chapter will discuss these points in detail while keeping the main focus on Buddha's techniques for personality development.

First, let us take a look at the criteria Buddha's society employed for personality evaluation. This observation will facilitate the understanding of what Buddha himself recommended for the same purpose. He observed that his society was using a number of irrational measurements to rate people as higher or lower. Sonadanda, who visited Buddha, summed up those weak criteria while explaining his own assessment of people. He told Buddha that one's birth into a noble family, knowledge about sacred texts, handsomeness, fair complexion, and stately appearance would fulfill the most important requirements for a strong personality.[1]

According to Buddha, however, these widely held beliefs would clearly sideline the more worthwhile criteria of an attractive personality. He not only rejected such weak building blocks of personality but also introduced solid values that would make an individual genuinely admirable and attractive.

Individual actions as the basis for personality evaluation

The central point in Buddha's argument regarding personality development is that great personalities are made, not inherited. "Birth does not make one a respectable person; one's action alone makes one a respectable person," he remarked.[2] The word "birth" refers to anything one might inherit: family background, wealth, physical appearance, race, caste, and so on. With regard to personality evaluation, these factors provide only fragile criteria. In contrast, "action" grants an individual solid material to construct an exceedingly attractive personality.

The word "action" conveys a broad meaning. "An action means what is done intentionally through words, deeds, and thoughts," Buddha explained.[3] Throughout the *Sutta Pitaka*, he made it clear that action should include both the external and internal behavior of the individual. He emphasized that, in order to develop an admirable personality, we should constantly modify our behavior patterns: physical actions and words, as well as thoughts.

With these remarks, Buddha affirmed our ability to shape our behavior, thus giving us the responsibility to develop our personalities. Some forms of behavior, of course, could be inborn, or "based on *kamma*," as Buddha called it. Still, human ability to influence inborn behavior has achieved a prominent position in Buddha's teaching. We may find it impossible to change ourselves completely in order to become altogether different people. Nevertheless, with self-awareness and observation, we may drastically improve our own behavior, an achievement that would result in our having more pleasing personalities.

As previously mentioned, personality development is a process, according to Buddha. A close analysis shows that this process consists of three steps. Let us examine each of them separately in order to facilitate this discussion.

Step 1: Reflect upon and identify your own behavior

The first step toward developing an admirable personality is to reflect upon and identify one's own behavior. We need to look into our own words, deeds, and thoughts and clearly recognize them. "An action with the body, speech, and mind should be done after repeated reflection," Buddha stated. "It [self-reflection] is similar to a man or a woman looking into a clear mirror or a bowl of clear water. If the person sees dust or a blemish on his or her face, he or she strives to get rid of it."[4] So, self-reflection means a true effort to look into our own actions with the hope of modifying our behavior.

For some of us, this task is the hardest. We may exhibit expert skill in exposing others' weaknesses but find it extremely difficult to detect our own. People often point their forefinger at others and say, "You are wrong!" but rarely point their thumb at themselves to make the same accusation:

> One sees others' weaknesses very easily but finds it very difficult to see one's own. One can expose others' mistakes just as a winnower blows away chaff from grain. Yet one hides one's own mistakes just as a hunter camouflages himself with small branches and leaves.[5]

These words of Buddha elucidate our failure to observe our own weaknesses. Inability to reflect on our own behavior hampers the process of adding pleasant qualities to our personalities.

Buddha noticed that this weakness is the main reason why some people remain stagnant in their personality development. Inability to recognize one's own mistake or weakness is the most obvious characteristic of a *bala*, a technical word meaning "inadequately developed person."[6] Having failed at the very initial stage, such a person shows little ability to improve his or her behavior.

Honest self-reflection versus escapism

Buddha cited angry resistance and denial as common forms of escapism that prevent people from seeing their faulty behavior. *Bala Vagga* in the *Anguttara Nikaya* consistently emphasized this point. Upon recognizing a mistake, these people would "show agitation, anger, and denial" instead of accepting it.[7] Inevitably, such individuals fail to make a genuine reflection upon their behavior.

These forms of self-defense are either absent or minimal in those who tend to make a true self-reflection. Such people do not hide their faulty behavior "just as a hunter camouflages himself with small branches and leaves." With sincerity and courage, they succeed in detecting the presence of various traits in their characters.

Anumana Sutta mentioned that close and honest self-investigation is the key to identifying the traits that would otherwise go unnoticed. "Am I so-and-so?" or "Do I possess such and such traits?" are the questions we need to ask ourselves in order to facilitate our clear insight. As Buddha instructed, "Self should be reflected upon self in this manner: 'Do I disparage others and exalt myself [while communicating]?'"[8] The same Sutta cited over fifteen characteristics, both wholesome and unwholesome, to be reflected upon in a similar way. Among these are the presence of immoral desires, the growth of jealousy within, and angry reaction to suggestions. This reflection would help one to "find the presence of unwholesome states [faulty behavior] that one must strive to get rid of," and the wholesome states that one should improve.[9] So, genuine self-reflection leads us to right self-understanding, the next important step to self-adjustment.

In Buddha's teaching, self-reflection leading to self-understanding is a vital phase in self-improvement. Genuine reflection on our own words, deeds, and thoughts allows us to identify our behavior. In other words, self-reflection answers the question "How do I react to my sensory experiences and mental images through words, actions, thoughts, and feelings?" With the ability to reflect on our own internal and external behavior, we correctly recognize our actions and thoughts. As explained in *Satipatthana Sutta,* the honest observer "sees lustful thought as lustful thought . . . and hateful thought as hateful thought."[10] Unbiased, impartial identification of our own words, deeds, and thoughts is the basic objective of self-reflection.

Step 2: Evaluate your own behavior

Buddha explained that self-evaluation should follow self-reflection. While self-reflection facilitates the detection of various individual characteristics, correct self-evaluation takes us further: it allows us to measure the value of these traits. This step is important because we also need to measure what we have observed within ourselves. Such a measurement would help us to decide whether a certain behavior we exhibit is pleasant or unpleasant to others.

This phase, again, may mislead us. We may quickly judge others' unpleasant behavior as wrong and repulsive but our own wrong actions as pleasant and relevant. For instance, when others dominate a conversation, we might say that they are listening to their own voice, but when we speak too much, we believe, of course, that we are providing very useful information and instructions. When others express anger, they exhibit rude behavior, but our own angry outburst is the most appropriate response in the situation. These self-favored conclusions indicate that correct self-evaluation can be tricky and needs careful observation.

Techniques for correct self-evaluation

Buddha recommended useful techniques to rate our own actions. As previously discussed, the purpose of self-reflection is to detect the presence of certain behavior within ourselves. The purpose of self-evaluation is to assess these behavior patterns. The *Sutta Pitaka* introduced the following methods for successful self-evaluation:

Technique 1: Let us examine our own response to others' behavior

Awareness of our own response to others' behavior, from Buddha's point of view, is a dependable approach for evaluating others' response to our own behavior. According to this method, first we need to examine the behavior patterns of various individuals. Importantly, this examination does not mean we should interfere with what others do. Rather, it means we should evaluate our own behavior in the light of others' actions. We may select different people and silently observe and evaluate their notable behavior patterns. For example, Buddha said:

> That person who praises himself or herself and disparages others is displeasing and disagreeable to me. Similarly, if I praise myself and disparage others, I would also be displeasing and disagreeable to others.[11]

In this example we come to the correct conclusion that our own display of ourselves and belittlement of others would be unpleasant since others' display of similar behavior is unpleasant to us. We are more likely to misjudge if we try to evaluate our own behavior independently. A comparative evaluation, in contrast, would offer us a great opportunity to determine social reaction to our own behavior.

Buddha cited a large number of human characteristics, either admirable or contemptible, to be observed and evaluated in this manner. As exemplified in the quotation given above, we may first detect the presence of these behaviors in different individuals and then examine our own inner response to such behavior. If we deem these actions to be unpleasant, our own display of similar behavior will also earn the same negative response from society. On the other hand, if we tend to admire a certain behavior of others, our own adoption of similar behavior would also receive a similar appreciation from society.

Technique 2: Let us identify our own mental states that cause pleasant and unpleasant behaviors

Recognition of mental states that prompt both pleasant and unpleasant behaviors is another way to evaluate our own actions. According to this approach, we need to examine the background of our behaviors and detect the urge behind them. Buddha identified all human actions as originating from six common sources: desire for sensory satisfaction, destructive urge, illusion, generosity, compassion, and right understanding. The first three of these mental states can trigger unpleasant actions while the other three bring about pleasant behavior. Our ability to identify these mental states during an action helps us differentiate between what is pleasant and what is unpleasant.

A question such as "Why do I want to do this or say this?" would facilitate the detection of the motive behind an action. For instance, when a strong urge persuades us to talk about ourselves, we might pause for a moment to ask what the inner motive would be. An honest observation would perhaps reveal that a futile effort to gain power over our listeners would be the actual motive. In this case, we are urged by greed, an unwholesome motive that manifests itself in different forms. Talking about ourselves, of course, is not always an effort to gain power. Still, words, as well as actions, can often emerge from our inner desire to be more powerful. Mindfulness about the motive behind an action clearly helps us to evaluate the forthcoming actions.

Technique 3: Let us examine the suitability of our actions

An evaluation of the appropriateness of our actions toward certain persons and in certain situations is another useful technique to assess our behavior. Buddha remarked that, even though he knew something to be true, he would not speak it at the wrong time.[12] He made a clear distinction between natural and rational behavior. Inner urge to do something is the natural force of behavior. Ability to evaluate the consequences of an action means the use of rationality. A person expecting to develop pleasant behavior should use the power of reasoning to evaluate his or her actions instead of giving in to instinct. The following words of Buddha clarify this point:

> When you are desirous of doing something through speech, you should reflect thus. Is this action unskilled? Does it lead to anguish? Is its result anguish . . . for myself and others? Does this action show my inner skill or lead to happiness . . . for myself and others?[13]

In everyday communications, we may have many "desirous" actions: to talk about our own achievements, to help others correct their behavior problems, or to say "Shut up!" to a grumbler. However, what positive effects should we expect by doing so? Unwholesome consequences lurk behind most of these "desirous" actions. Undoubtedly, we would earn a low personality evaluation from our listeners since our behavior would appear unpleasant to them. An assessment of our actions in terms of their effects would avoid a negative reaction from the listener.

As mentioned above, Buddha clarified that, even though something is actually true, he would not speak the truth to the wrong audience at the wrong time. He also instructed his disciples to follow the same principle. One may argue that the truth is the truth, and that we should speak it irrespective of the occasion and the nature of the audience. However, Buddha explained that speaking the truth to the wrong person or at the wrong time would cause a negative reaction. Therefore, we need to examine the suitability of our words before we decide to speak. The same measurement should be applied to evaluate other forms of actions as well.

Step 3: Use self-evaluation to adjust and improve behavior

So far, we have discussed Buddha's teaching that self-reflection and self-evaluation are two gradual and connected steps toward personality development. The final phase of this process is self-adjustment and improvement.

Self-evaluation has already given us a clear picture of where adjustment and improvement are necessary. Now we need to acquire the qualities that make us more pleasant to others, and to maintain those pleasant qualities we have already acquired. Sariputta's explanation of Buddha's words clarifies this step:

> It [self-improvement] is similar to the thinking of a young man or woman who has checked his or her reflection in a clear and pure mirror or in a bowl of clear water. If the person sees dust or blemish on his or her face, he or she strives to get rid of it. If the person sees no dust or blemish, he or she feels happy and thinks, "Indeed, it is good for me; I am clean." Similarly, if you, while reflecting, see unwholesome states, you should strive to get rid of them. If you see they no longer exist, you should be delighted, and determined to maintain the developed states.[14]

So, effort plays a key role in helping us to develop and retain pleasant qualities. In the same way that a young person is careful about his or her appearance, we need to be careful about our own behavior. If elated with our own "beautiful" actions, we may make further efforts to improve ourselves. If disappointed with unpleasant actions, we should make a determined effort to curb them. Without making an effort, we would find that the chances of acquiring an attractive personality are remote.

In a society in which people look for easy success and instant results, the word "effort" might seem unappealing. Buddha, in fact, saw no instant achievement in the matter of personality development. As with success in most fields, construction of a pleasant personality requires individual effort. However, this effort does not mean a person's withdrawal from other work and total concentration on personality development alone. A few simple but productive habits will yield excellent results. Let us look at Buddha's recommendations.

Practice imitation and elimination

Buddha constantly praised imitation and elimination as greatly effective practices for developing an admirable personality. Imitation means following others: we may make an effort to acquire their attractive behavior. Elimination means refraining from following others: we may strive to leave out their unpleasant behavior. This chapter has already discussed how to observe and evaluate others' behavior.

Right evaluation allows us to decide what is to be followed or left out. Here is an example:

> "That person who is stubborn and arrogant is disagreeable and displeasing to me. If I were stubborn and arrogant, I would also be disagreeable and displeasing to others." When you gain this knowledge, you must make up your mind and think, "I will not be stubborn and arrogant."[15]

This example shows the process of imitation and elimination. The behavior of people in society constantly highlights the characteristics that we need to adopt or reject. As spectators, we evaluate others' behavior and constantly change and modify our own behavior patterns, thus making us more acceptable to others.

Some might argue that they are independent and are capable of learning by themselves rather than through imitating others. Self-reliance, of course, is an admirable characteristic in Buddha's teaching, but, realistically, no human being can improve his or her behavior without observing others. In fact, imitation and elimination is a lifelong process that everyone follows without even realizing it. Buddha instructed us to imitate or eliminate certain behaviors of others selectively, after careful observation and evaluation.

Restrain some behavior

Similar to imitation and elimination, self-restraint, according to Buddha, further facilitates self-adjustment. *Sila* signifies self-restraint, which, in simple terms, means our ability to grapple with our tendency to exhibit unpleasant and unsuitable behavior. When we identify the rise of unwholesome mental states within ourselves, self-restraint successfully stops us from displaying the consequent behavior. Similarly, when we find our desired actions to be unsuitable, self-restraint again comes to our rescue. We constantly develop pleasant behavior, thanks to this time-honored development technique.

Importantly, we should not define self-restraint as suppression, which means forceful and painful hiding of behavior. As already discussed, self-reflection and self-evaluation are the forerunners of self-restraint. In other words, we tend to restrain ourselves after obtaining a right understanding about our own behavior. Self-restraint emerges as an effect of right understanding, not as a forceful suppression of actions.

For example, let us discuss how we restrain ourselves from reacting angrily. Self-reflection and self-evaluation, the precursors to self-restraint, have already given us a clear understanding about the angry feelings we are experiencing. An angry expression would be the natural reaction, but we are mindful of the unwholesome mental state we are in. That awareness would indicate to us that an angry reaction would hardly be pleasant. With right knowledge facilitating the effort, we restrain unpleasant behavior without force or pain.

In another way, self-restraint means gaining the upper hand over natural behavior. Even though we think naturally, we need to behave rationally in order to construct an attractive personality. Self-restraint paves the way to that end.

Strive for inner development

The two practices discussed above—imitation or elimination, and self-restraint—focus on our external behavior, to help us cultivate pleasant actions and weed out unpleasant actions. Apart from this approach, Buddha emphasized inner development as a unique step in acquiring pleasing qualities. He said, "When mind is protected, you protect all of your actions."[16] The fully developed person is the one who has improved not only external behavior but also thoughts, feelings, and attitudes.[17]

Buddha clarified that enhancement of external behavior patterns is an essential but inadequate step in developing an admirable personality. Pleasant words and deeds, of course, make us socially acceptable, but improvement of attitudes and thoughts clearly confirms our social acceptability. "Actions and words originating from a developed mind bring happiness," Buddha stated.[18] His assertion is that we need to work on our inner development in order to raise our personality development to the best possible level.

On the one hand, development of external behavior itself contributes to inner development. In other words, when we acquire new external behavior patterns, we tend to internalize them. For instance, as we use pleasant words, we begin to feel that we should continue to use them. Buddha highlighted this point by citing the connection between *sila* (behavior development) and *panna* (wisdom). According to Buddha's teaching, we fail to develop wisdom if we do not develop verbal and physical behavior. External behavior development tends to facilitate inner development.

In addition, Buddha also recommended useful techniques for inner development itself. The word *bhavana* denotes the techniques he recommended for this purpose. Enhancement of loving-kindness and wisdom within us is the most effective way to improve inner development. *Bhavana* prepares us to be in accordance with our modified external behavior. For instance, to say "I am sorry to hear you were in trouble" would show improved external behavior. To feel compassion toward the person who was in trouble would indicate actual inner development. Right behavior without right thoughts may be helpful in constructing an admirable personality; right behavior with right thoughts is essential to make our personality development more complete.

The next chapter, which focuses on happiness, will discuss important *bhavana* techniques that help inner development. These topics are so interrelated that we can hardly separate them. While improvement of inner behavior supports personality development, the same improvement also plays a crucial role in making a person happy and peaceful. So, the chapter about happiness seems to be the right place for *bhavana*.

Summary

Buddha's teaching allows us to develop charming characters that would earn appreciation and respect. He recommended a methodical approach to personality development. This approach consists of three steps: self-reflection, self-evaluation, and self-adjustment. Personality development means both the modification of our external behavior (words and deeds) and the improvement of our internal behavior (thoughts, feelings, and attitudes). We can modify our words and physical actions through imitation, elimination, and self-restraint. Inner development is possible through *bhavana* methods, which are popularly known as meditation.

Chapter Fourteen

Toward Lasting Happiness

Indeed we live happily. In the midst of worried people, we live free from worry. . . . Happiness is the greatest wealth.

Buddha, the *Dhammapada*

The trek through thirteen chapters has finally brought us to the all-important topic: Buddha's guidance to happiness in life. The immeasurable importance of this topic lies in the following truth: wealth, family, career, or anything else that contributes to one's success serves little purpose if it fails to make one happy. "I have seen no other important acquisition for a person than happiness," Buddha noted.[1] Happiness is the highest achievement in our effort to be successful. As Buddha repeatedly emphasized, we must search for a stable and intense form of happiness, find it, and keep it with us in order to make success genuinely meaningful.

For several strong reasons, we can trust Buddha's ability to lead us toward this end. As he repeatedly stressed, Buddha's sole endeavor throughout his life was to find happiness, and, after considerable trial and error, he proclaimed that he had found it. The most reliable sources indicate that his words, deeds, and thoughts reflected a consistent and intense happiness.

Having observed his simple life, one visitor wondered whether Buddha had rejected happiness. In reply, Buddha said, "If there are any individuals in this world experiencing happiness, I am, undoubtedly, one of them."[2] He further remarked in the same Sutta that he was happier than most people who possessed material wealth and power. Unlike some of his contemporaries who sought happiness, Buddha did not make himself suffer while anticipating happiness in a later life. Instead, he experienced it throughout his life, thus highlighting his credibility as a reliable guide to our own happiness.

His disciples' joyful utterances about their own happiness further justify Buddha's ability to lead us to happiness. We have two ancient books, *Theragatha* and *Therigatha*, containing the poetic utterances of Buddha's male and female disciples. Happiness is the theme that pervades all these utterances. Those disciples did not have luxury or expensive material possessions, but they had one possession in common: great happiness. Buddha successfully guided thousands of his disciples to happiness, and we can be confident that his instructions will do the same for us.

Furthermore, if we fail to make ourselves happy after following the teaching of Buddha, we miss the most important achievement he wanted us to have. Advising the first group of Bhikkhus he had trained, Buddha remarked:

> Go earnestly from place to place for the benefit of the many, *for the happiness of the many*, explaining to people the teaching that is excellent at the beginning, excellent in the middle, and excellent at the end.[3]

Obviously, the word "happiness" indicates Buddha's ultimate objective of asking his disciples to take his message to society. He earnestly intended to make people happy, and he knew that his teaching could serve that purpose.

Scientific evidence

Available scientific evidence clearly justifies our reliance on Buddha as our guide to inner peace. Even though we do not have to depend on experiments to have confidence in Buddha's teaching, they provide relevant information and reinforce our claim. In a widely publicized news item, global media such as BBC and CNN reported on two separate studies done in late 2003 in American universities. According to these reports, the researchers found evidence to suggest that followers of Buddha's teaching are actually happy—in fact, they are happier than most. New scanning techniques have revealed that "certain areas of the brain light up constantly" in those who practice Buddhist meditation.[4] This finding suggests their positive emotions and pleasant moods. One study, in particular, found that the left prefrontal lobes—the area that is connected to positive emotions, self-control, and temperament—constantly lit up in experienced Buddhist practitioners.

Consequently, researchers at the University of California San Francisco Medical Center said that followers of Buddha "were less likely to be shocked, flustered, surprised, or as angry compared to other people."[5] Paul Ekman, the research leader, has reportedly said, "The most reasonable hypothesis is that there is something about conscientious Buddhist practice that results in the kind of happiness we all seek."[6] All this evidence leads to the conclusion that Buddha's teaching guides us to the most valued mental achievement: lasting happiness.

Initial preparation

Yet, how do we bless ourselves with this most fulfilling accomplishment? To answer this question, we need to go through a step-by-step process rather than rely on an instant solution. First, we need to have a clear understanding about ourselves. The question "Who am I?" requires the correct answer. Our ancestors' misleading answers to this question seem to have been a crucial factor that prevented numerous generations from seeing the path to happiness.

Buddha identified *I* as a free individual, one who should take the entire responsibility of making oneself happy. *I* is an embodiment of potential and skill to make *I* happy; no one other than *I* can make *I* happy. "Self-improvement or self-impairment is one's own task; someone does not improve another."[7] Buddha does not make anybody happy, but "only shows the path to happiness."[8] Essentially, as a preparation for the achievement of happiness, we first need to take the responsibility for our own happiness.

Notably, self-confidence, the strong faith in one's own ability to make oneself happy, plays a vital role in this initial phase. As previously discussed, Buddha rejected three forms of speculative thought that were believed to make a person happy or unhappy. To facilitate the present discussion, we may repeat them here:

1. The actions one did in past lives solely determine one's happiness or unhappiness in the present life.
2. Divine power solely determines one's happiness or unhappiness.
3. Mere chance determines one's happiness or unhappiness.[9]

Having rejected these extremist views, Buddha stressed one's own ability to make oneself happy. Those who adhere to the views listed above deny their own ability to make themselves content and peaceful. Buddha unequivocally promoted the view that, despite individual differences, any person possesses the ability to make himself or herself happy. In other words, we need to be aware that *I* possesses the enormous ability to make *I* happy.

Scientific research on experienced Buddhist practitioners again confirms the accuracy of this statement. In late 2004, a team of researchers at the University of Wisconsin-Madison experimented on the brain activity of meditators introduced by the Dalai Lama. These researchers discovered a dramatic increase of gamma waves in the brains, particularly in the left prefrontal cortex, of these experienced practitioners. Gamma waves suggest brain activity. Their presence in that particular area of the cortex indicates positive emotions. Referring to the meditation practitioners, Richard Davidson, the research leader, commented, "Their mental practice is having an effect on the brain in the same way golf or tennis practice will enhance performance."[10]

Another experiment conducted in Tibet in early 2005 with the participation of monks who practiced meditation provides more evidence to reconfirm this statement. The researchers have found that "meditation can literally change the way Buddhist monks see the world."[11] They came to this conclusion after finding the capacity of the monks to stimulate the left side of the brain, the area associated with happiness, even in the presence of unhappy visual experiences.

These experiments indicate that we can change our brain structure and function, especially through the practice of meditation. We need to be aware that we have the potential to develop our minds, and are in a position to take responsibility for our own happiness.

A few attitudinal changes within ourselves grant us self-confidence to undertake this responsibility. One of the areas that needs attention in this regard is the memory of unpleasant actions and experiences from our past. Since such actions and experiences continue to disturb our inner peace, happiness constantly eludes us. Buddha's advice is that we should not allow these thoughts to disturb us. "Let the past be gone," he advised. "Now" is the right time that *I* should begin life.[12] Whatever mistakes we made in the past pose no hindrance if we earnestly start the search for happiness now:

> Having been negligent in the past,
> One later becomes diligent.
> That person brightens the world
> Similar to the moon emerging from behind the clouds.[13]

This simile says it all: the soothing moonlight is the inner happiness one experiences after leaving behind the unpleasant past. That inner brightness not only makes the person happy but also allows others to be happy. Essentially, in our effort to discover true happiness, we should first cleanse the corrupted memory: we should let unpleasant memories go, and determine to move ahead, beginning afresh.

Buddha observed that, similar to the worries buried in the past, apprehension about our future also tends to weaken the happiness we are experiencing. Therefore, we need to free ourselves from such feelings in order to prepare ourselves for a blissful present. When Buddha urged his followers to leave aside the unpleasant past, he asked them to stop worrying about the future as well. Clarifying this point, he further said:

> Brooding over the future
> And repenting the past,
> The unwise wither like a green reed
> Cut down and left in the sun.[14]

This poetic expression indicates that some people tend to breed sorrow while thinking about their future. Perhaps their fear of the future causes this situation. They suffer intensely, just as an uprooted reed (bamboo plant) dries up in the sun. Appropriately, the kind of reed Buddha mentioned is *Nala*, which grows in shaded, watery areas. If separated from the stem and left in the sun, this reed finds itself in an utterly helpless situation, presenting a very pitiable sight. Similarly, one who unnecessarily worries about the future finds it impossible to achieve inner peace.

Buddha specifically instructed his followers to think that "the [unpleasant] past is dead and gone, and the future is yet to come."[15] Therefore, rumination on unpleasant past experiences and apprehension of the future serve no purpose to the person who strives to live a happy life. "Begin now" is Buddha's advice. One should know that *I* can live happily if *I* now begins to follow the steps that are essential to happiness.

Next, the fresh beginning needs reinforcement. Buddha's phrase "dwelling in happiness" does not suggest a secondary objective; it is the primary and the foremost objective in life. The wise person, aware that "I am dear to myself," should take all precautionary actions for self-protection.[16] The word "protection" means the shield against the disturbances that affect our inner peace. *I* is the person who shields the mind of *I* from such disturbances. Constant mindfulness plays a predominant role at this crucial juncture. We need to be constantly mindful about our own resolution to make ourselves happy. We need to repeat to ourselves, "I am not going to allow anybody or anything to steal my happiness."

Of course, if we allow others to destroy our happiness, we present ourselves as ordinary and unsuccessful people. How can we rate ourselves as successful if we fail to retain the most precious thing in our life! The advice Buddha offered to his ordained disciples seems to work for others as well. He reminded them to be "watchful while walking, standing, sitting, and lying down." Striving to keep our own happiness undiminished, we also need to be constantly watchful about invasive thoughts that might hamper our inner peace. "I am happy, and I should keep myself happy" is a mantra that needs frequent repeating.

Then begins the real action, which consists of easy-to-follow techniques. Of course, the initiation of most beneficial tasks needs effort; so does the beginning of "dwelling in happiness." Nevertheless, most experienced practitioners may agree that, after a shaky beginning, they have succeeded in their effort. A careful study of the *Sutta Pitaka* reveals the following seven steps that allow us to reach an elevated and stable form of happiness.

Step 1: Avoid entertaining mind-created answers to everyday experiences

Buddha identified mind-created reactions to everyday experiences as a major obstruction to happiness. In *Madhupindika Sutta,* his chief disciple Sariputta explained this mental process clearly. He clarified how people attach their own meanings to their sensory experiences and, by doing so, how they experience unhappiness. "One reproduces and enlarges what one reasons about," he remarked. "As a result, one allows such thoughts to attack oneself."[17]

This Sutta explained a deep but regular psychological process that tends to keep our inner peace at bay. Human nature urges us to interpret sensory experiences, but these interpretations often depend on assumptions rather than on facts. The technical Pali word used to identify the so-called interpretation is *papanceti*. This word means "grow within," or "enlarge in the mind." This psychological process often tends to hurt the person rather than to benefit him or her. "Attack" means this inner disturbance.

The following sentence will exemplify this mentality:

He didn't smile because he doesn't like me.

In this sentence, the claim is a true visual experience, but the reason that supports the claim is clearly a mental creation rather than an actual one. The instant aftermath of this reaction is unhappiness. Being watchful, one may observe how quickly one's happy mood would take a reverse turn when these negative assumptions interfere.

Worst of all, the mind does not stop there but continues to create more "why" questions and more "because" answers. "Why doesn't he like me?" one would ask next, and the answer would appear instantly: "Because he thinks I am stupid." This process goes on and on, only to worsen the misery that has already settled in the mind.

Of course, assumptions are important for finding right answers to various questions. However, according to Buddha's teaching, the belief that assumptions are true neither leads us to right answers nor makes us happy. In the example discussed above, for instance, the actual reason why he did not smile could be altogether different. Through our own experience, we have understood that, when in a thoughtful mood, people miss visual objects and, when in an unhappy mood, they fail to be cheerful. The person who did not smile may have been in such a situation when the other person saw him. His cheerful appearance the next day would convince the speaker that he or she was quite mistaken, but the unhappiness caused by misjudged reasons has already taken its toll.

Sariputta explained that people attach meanings to their experiences and, consequently, tend to create unhappy moods even when objects are not present to their senses. Depending on past experiences stored in memory, people create imaginary pictures only to drag themselves into unhappy territory. "Thoughts [also] arise as a result of mind and [mere] mental objects," remarked Sariputta, while explaining the connection between senses and sensual objects.[18] These thoughts also go through a process of evaluation, which eventually would influence the person's mood in a negative way.

We may look into ourselves to find out how true this statement is. On a peaceful day, we may suddenly find ourselves trapped by an unhappy thought coming out of nowhere. These thoughts occur as we mentally retrieve our past experiences and reevaluate the unpleasant meanings attached to those experiences. Consequently, we deprive ourselves of the inner peace with which we began the day. In reality, however, neither these experiences nor their meanings exist anywhere other than in our minds. How irrational it is to let a nonexistent experience destroy happiness, the most precious thing in our life!

Buddha's teaching encourages us to refrain from clinging to self-created meanings given to sensual objects. Especially, as we recognize a sound or a sight or remember a similar experience in the past, we should see it as it is, not as something to be expanded with self-invented causes. This practice would contribute immensely to the happiness we are all looking for.

Step 2: Let go of greed and malice

We have already discussed greed and malicious thoughts in detail, but we return to this topic in order to highlight its relationship to happiness. Buddha saw nothing more detrimental to happiness than these two forms of mental reaction. "Greed breeds unhappiness; greed breeds fear," he said. "When greed ceases to exist, no unhappiness or fear exists."[19] Referring to malice, he mentioned that those who eliminate it "live happily and peacefully among the haters."[20] The *Sutta Pitaka* constantly repeated Buddha's emphasis that absence of greed and malice in the mind makes us exceedingly happy.

Still, people fail, or rather do not make a serious effort, to have control over greed and malicious thoughts in real life. They give way to these two natural urges repeatedly. The human mind, according to Buddha, is brilliant in its basic form but becomes polluted as a result of its contact with the external world.[21] Nothing other than greed and malice can do more to pollute the human mind and cloud its natural happiness.

Awareness of the mind's tendencies is the first step in achieving peace of mind. "When a lustful thought occurs, one should know that it is a lustful thought," Buddha instructed.[22] Similarly, we need to be vigilant about other thoughts, feelings, and emotions that occur in our minds.[23] The main reason for most people's failure to curb greed and malicious thought is their inability to recognize the presence of these forces in their minds. Driven by these urges, many unknowingly allow their feelings and emotions to control them. In contrast, when they detect the presence of these unwholesome thoughts within, they know what to do next.

Having detected and recognized this inner tendency, we should next repeat to ourselves what has happened to us. This step allows us to control the undesirable emotion. "I am angry; I am angry," an ill-tempered person has to repeat to himself or herself, for instance. This practice, of course, seems to be the most difficult part in the entire process. Without a genuine effort, we may allow our inner feelings to take a firm grip on ourselves instead of managing to take hold of the feeling itself. However, those who make a purposeful attempt succeed in their effort and take a giant step forward: they prevent themselves from being taken into an unhappy state. They understand that the departure from burning desire and anger-dominated thoughts is soothing indeed for the mind.

Step 3: Pursue a goal and enjoy achieving it

While Buddha identified a greedy action as a forerunner of inner suffering, he recognized pursuit of a goal and the consequent achievement of it as a clear basis for individual happiness. The term *atthi sukha* indicates this source of happiness. As it was defined in the *Anguttara Nikaya*, *atthi sukha* suggests the happy thoughts derived from achieving material success through just means. In a broader sense, any form of success achieved through rightful means is a source of happiness, according to Buddha.

To understand the difference between a greed-motivated action and a goal, we need to evaluate both in terms of their objectives. In basic terms, a greedy action disregards the well-being of others while overemphasizing one's own sensory satisfaction. A goal, in contrast, relies on one's own potential, and its achievement brings benefits for oneself and others. Buddha clearly stressed that such an achievement does make us happy.

We may look at Buddha's own life to understand the truth of this statement. He strove for seven years to attain enlightenment, the most noteworthy objective in his life. After a strenuous endeavor that symbolized the fruitfulness of human effort, he eventually attained his objective. What did he do immediately afterward? For three weeks he remained in solitude and enjoyed his remarkable achievement. He derived great happiness from thinking about what many people dreamed about, but that only he had attained.

Again, in one of his discourses given in later years, Buddha looked back to contemplate another achievement that gave him immense satisfaction. He reviewed the remarkable feat he had achieved during the forty-five years since his enlightenment:

> I am now old . . . I have come to the end of my journey. Yet, I have senior, experienced, skillful . . . Bhikkhus, laymen, and laywomen. This society is successful, prosperous, widespread, and popular . . . I don't see any teacher who has reached such a renowned position as I am in.[24]

What Buddha achieved between his enlightenment and his death seems to be one of the greatest achievements by a single human being during his or her lifetime. Not only did he establish a progressive new society within the traditional, rigid Vedic society, but he also convinced most traditionalists to abandon their beliefs and practices and to join his new society. He profoundly influenced people's ways of thinking and brought about drastic social changes. The quotation cited above shows his rightful appreciation of his great achievement. He happily visualized what he had begun in his mid-thirties, and then achieved several decades later.

Obviously, the word "achievement" does not mean the completion of a gigantic task that only a sprinkling of people would be capable of. From Buddha's point of view, "achievement" means any accomplishment associated with either inner development or social success. Most of Buddha's ordained disciples regarded their spiritual development—their ability to handle greed, malice, and illusion—as their highest achievement. This accomplishment gave them a stable form of happiness throughout their lives. The members of his lay community also obtained a similar form of happiness by thinking over their own meaningful lives, which, from Buddha's point of view, was a notable achievement.

Specifically for the lay community, Buddha stated that financial success is an achievement that would bring happiness upon reflection. As already discussed, *atthi sukha* means "the happiness derived from thinking over the achievements in the field of money and wealth." This achievement may include not only the wealth one has accumulated with right effort but also the knowledge and skill one developed in order to gain financial strength. An educational qualification that would enhance one's financial stability, for instance, belongs to this category. One may think of the milestones on one's way to financial strength as a source of happiness.

We observe that reflection upon a greed-driven action done in the past would hardly make us happy, while visualization of an achievement would rarely fail to please us. A greedy action—overindulgence in sensory satisfaction, for instance—is gone, and an effort to refresh the mind with such an action would yield only an uneasy emptiness. The achievement of a worthwhile goal remains with us and becomes a source of enjoyment.

Step 4: Look at others' unpleasant actions with compassion

Buddha also maintained that our own compassionate attitude toward people who exhibit some noisome behavior would help us stabilize our own inner peace. When the destructive urge slowly leaves us, two notable changes take place inside. First, anger, hatred, and other related feelings and emotions lose their grip within us. Next, the mind opens its gates for compassionate feelings to pour in. We realize that the people who previously appeared so noisome to us now deserve our compassion. This realization further strengthens our inner peace.

This statement does not suggest that those who commit an inhuman action should be tolerated, and that the related consequences should be ignored. Clearly, Buddha endeavored throughout his life to change human actions that caused unwholesome consequences. Such topics as social discrimination and violence never escaped his attention. He argued assertively and convincingly against such practices, and successfully launched a huge campaign in order to change them. In other words, Buddha never advocated tolerance of harmful human behavior as a way to keep our mind at peace.

However, we observe that what destroy our inner peace on a daily basis are not crime, corruption, and malpractice in society, but the trivial experiences in our day-to-day life. A speeding driver cutting into our lane, a coworker rarely having a happy face, or a roommate failing to wash the dishes may disturb us more than a heinous crime in the city would. Of course, people should improve, and their unpleasant behavior should change, however trivial it appears to be. Yet, taking these relatively trivial actions into our own hearts would only ruin the happiness that we are all entitled to.

Therefore, following Buddha's advice, we rightly view the actions of those people compassionately instead of allowing them to destroy our own happiness. A speeding driver cuts abruptly into our lane because he or she may be in a hurry. Perhaps we are actually driving too slowly in the fast lane, from that driver's point of view. A roommate did not wash the dishes because, having final exams the next day, he or she forgot to do so. Perhaps he or she is still inexperienced where social etiquette is concerned. These reasons may help us to have a sort of understanding about others' actions. Such an understanding would facilitate our effort to develop a compassionate attitude toward those people.

Yet the most effective way to understand some people's unusually annoying behavior and, consequently, to feel compassion toward them, is to see them as imperfect human beings, just as we all are. Buddha pointed out that "mental imbalance" is one of the most notable occurrences among human beings. Every individual, according to his explanation, possesses some anomaly. Unawareness of this fact leads us to make a big mistake when we interpret some noisome human behavior: we believe that such behavior is deliberate and intentional.

For instance, a teacher may regard an average student's angry response to a low grade as an intentional insult. However, the truth might be that an emotional disorder activated the student's angry response, and that the student did not mean to insult the teacher. Biological factors control emotions and related physical actions, and some people seem to have an unusual weakness in controlling their emotions. This awareness gives us the knowledge that people exhibit intolerable behavior not because they mean to hurt others but because they have fallen prey to the chemical imbalance in their own bodies.

Of course, they must train themselves to behave well—and Buddha asserted that they can—but their failure to do so should not be allowed to rob us of our own peace of mind. As we learn to connect their weaknesses to their own biological factors, we not only understand those people but also tend to develop compassion toward them. This approach clearly protects our own peace of mind.

Practicing loving-kindness meditation seems to be a very effective habit for this purpose. Right understanding almost always gives rise to compassion. We understand that no reaction would be more appropriate than feeling compassion toward those who exhibit unpleasant behavior. So, we focus on those people and repeat to ourselves, "May you be well, happy, and peaceful!"

Nobody can guarantee that we can change others and make them happy. Yet, we should know that we possess enormous power to improve ourselves and make ourselves happy. A poetic utterance of Buddha sums up this attitude:

We live so happily
Among the people with inner difficulties.
We live as healthy ones
Among disturbed people.[25]

Step 5: Work for others' benefit

Buddha identified a clear myth that people still hold as a profound truth: the belief that the more one satisfies one's own senses, the happier one tends to be. Buddha discovered that the opposite of this belief would be the actual truth. He claimed that those who would fulfill their duties toward others, alleviate the suffering of others, and contribute to social progress would actually be the happy people.

As previously discussed, several of Buddha's contemporaries promoted the erroneous view that indulgence in sensory satisfaction would make people happy. Some of these "teachers" blatantly disregarded social ethics. They claimed that sensory satisfaction would be identical with happiness, but Buddha's key phrase *bhoga sukha* (happiness gained through the usage of wealth) clarifies his opposition to this mistaken view. From his viewpoint, one can achieve happiness by using one's wealth not only for oneself but also for others.

According to this clarification, we can derive great satisfaction by fulfilling our duties to parents, children, friends, and others. Of course, Buddha reminded us that we should not neglect our own well-being, but that attention to others' well-being is a great source of happiness.

One may revive memories and ask oneself which of them make one happy. Memories of eating and drinking never come to the forefront. Other exciting experiences have departed, leaving an uneasy vacuum. However, what one has done for others provides a sense of self-fulfillment and a feeling of meaningfulness in life.

Parents are happy because they have guided their children to the highest possible level. Adult children are happy because they have fulfilled their obligations toward their aging parents. We are all happy because we have helped the needy, participated in volunteer work, or donated to a meaningful cause. What we do for others makes us genuinely happy.

Buddha observed that both *bhavana* and *dana* are great practices that lead us toward happiness. As discussed in the previous section, *bhavana* means "inner development," for which cultivation of compassion is a basic requirement. When compassion grows in the mind, happiness also shines. *Dana* (practice of generosity) is the external manifestation of compassion developed internally. If we are compassionate, we, undoubtedly, practice generosity. That practice also leads us to happiness, similar to what compassion does.

Step 6: Live a life full of principles

Buddha further elaborated that a principled life would grant us a great opportunity to find peace within ourselves. He used the term *anavajja sukha* to mean this important source of inner peace. On several occasions, Buddha remarked that we do not have to wait for the next life to receive the positive effects of our wholesome actions. By practicing uprightness, we can find inner peace in our present life. The Pali sentence *kathapunno idha nandati* symbolizes this teaching. *Kathapunno* is the person who lives a life full of principles, and such a person finds happiness in this very life (*idha nandati*).

Two questions await explanation at this point. First, what are the characteristics of the "person who lives a life full of principles"? Next, how does such a person achieve happiness?

We have three Pali words—*punna, kusala,* and *dhamma*—that convey basically the same meaning: disciplined and upright way of living. Throughout his life, Buddha strove to lead people to *punna, kusala,* or *dhamma* and to prevent them from practicing their opposites: *papa, akusala,* or *adhamma.* The following words spoken by one of Buddha's disciples convey Buddha's advice on living a principled life:

> Avoidance of unwholesome actions,
> Practice of wholesome actions,
> And development of the mind:
> This is what Buddha insists on.[26]

Principled life, then, means a combination of upright conduct and wholesome thought. With right evaluation, we refrain from doing unwholesome actions and speaking unwholesome words. We also carefully select the right actions and the right words. To match the modification of our external behavior, we strive to develop our thoughts. This effort epitomizes principled life.

Living such a life seems to connect to individual happiness more closely than one might expect. In fact, such actions provide a soothing experience to our mind. "A layperson lives his or her life with righteous words, righteous deeds, and righteous thoughts. By thinking about the righteous way of living, he or she derives happiness and inner peace," Buddha explained.[27] Perhaps righteous acts do not bring their fullest effects immediately, but in the long run their positive effects on our mental health become more manifest.

As Buddha further clarified, an intentional deed takes time to mature in our minds. The word he used was *paccati*. The terms *punnam paccati* and *papam paccati* mean that both wholesome and unwholesome actions gather momentum in the mind as time goes by. "When unwholesome actions done in the past gradually mature internally, the person experiences more unhappiness," claimed Buddha.[28] In contrast, a matured wholesome action makes the person exceedingly happy.

Maturation suggests development and firm establishment of such actions within ourselves. As we reflect on these actions, they grow and find a permanent place within us. While unpleasant actions begin to haunt us, wholesome actions continue to soothe us. Most people find that qualities such as their own truthfulness, generosity, and nonviolence pave the way for them to achieve peace of mind. Thus, our own noble principles grant us a dependable source of happiness.

Step 7: Accept inevitable changes as a part of natural law

Buddha emphasized human potential as a greatly effective factor in bringing about positive changes to human life. In other words, he stated that we possess the ability to change the physical world and to improve the quality of life. Buddha's advice to King Kosala that controlled eating would grant a person a long and healthy life[29] is just one example. However, Buddha did not present a totalizing theory. We cannot change everything, particularly the natural process of human life. Buddha explained that inner peace is attainable not by denying natural laws but by accepting them as inseparable from life.

At the very core of Buddha's philosophy, we find the teaching of impermanence (*anicca*). "The entire physical phenomenon is subject to change," remarked Buddha.[30] Realization of this truth is crucial to remaining unperturbed by various natural occurrences in life. Buddha said, "One who realizes the impermanence of all natural phenomena finds inner peace."[31]

Such conditions as disease, physical deterioration, death, and separation from loved ones, according to Buddha's classification, are a part of natural law. Of course, we can minimize or postpone these occurrences in our lives, but we can never stop them. Development of wisdom to accept these inevitable changes calmly is the only rational approach.

Buddha specifically encouraged his lay followers to see themselves as a part of nature instead of regarding their bodies as objects of attachment. Developed as a form of meditation, this attitude would allow us to realize and accept the inevitability of physical changes. Of course, Buddha never advised his lay disciples to develop a pessimistic attitude toward life. His aim was to pave the way for their inner peace amid such unavoidable conditions as sickness and physical deterioration.

Summary

Achievement of happiness, according to Buddha, should be the ultimate goal in life. He asserted that we should prioritize and take sole responsibility for our own happiness. The belief that greedy pursuit of pleasure grants us happiness is a social myth. The truth, in fact, is the opposite: reduced greed provides us a potent source of inner peace. Striving for success is completely different from chasing after greed. A personal achievement always remains with us to refresh our minds with pleasant thoughts. Such thoughts and actions as compassion, generosity, dutifulness, and upright conduct stand out as very effective practices to soothe our minds. After all, development of wisdom to accept inevitable changes in life makes our inner peace and happiness more complete.

Notes

Epigraph

Anguttara Nikaya III: Puggala Vagga: Andha Sutta; *Anguttara Nikaya X*: Akankha Vagga: Vaddhi Sutta

Note: The epigraph combines two separate sources. Buddha defined the wise layperson in Andha Sutta and talked about his lay followers' tenfold development in Vaddhi Sutta.

Chapter One

Epigraph taken from: *Anguttara Nikaya III*: Bharandu Vagga: Paticchanna Sutta

1. *Samyutta Nikaya 1*: Kosala Samyutta: Pancaraja Sutta
2. *Anguttara Nikaya II*: Sukha Vagga: 1-2
3. *Samyutta Nikaya IV*: Vedana Samyutta: Niramisa Sutta

Note: The term *samisa piti* has been translated as "happiness in worldly life." *Samisa* means "carnal" or "belonging to secular life." In this Sutta, Buddha repeats the same adjectives to describe sound, smell, taste, and physical contact. The translation avoids the repetitions.

4. *Samyutta Nikaya XI*: Sotapatti Samyutta: Veludvareyya Sutta

Chapter Two

Epigraph taken from: *Anguttara Nikaya VI*: Dhammika Vagga: Ina Sutta

1. *Anguttara Nikaya VIII*: Gotami Vagga: Vyagghapajja Sutta
2. *Samyutta Nikaya I*: Kosala Samyutta: Pathama Aputtaka Sutta
3. *Anguttara Nikaya IV*: Pattakamma Vagga: Anana Sutta
4. *Digha Nikaya 1*: 2: Samannaphala Sutta
5. Ibid.
6. *Digha Nikaya III*: 31: Sigalovada Sutta
7. *Anguttara Nikaya VIII*: Yamaka Vagga: Dutiya Sampada Sutta
8. *Digha Nikaya III*: 31: Sigalovada Sutta
9. *Anguttara Nikaya V*: Mundaraja Vagga: Pancabhoga Adiya Sutta

Note: The word *atithi* is generally translated as "visitors," but this translation is incorrect. Buddha, in this quotation, has already mentioned relatives, friends, and associates. One finds no other "visitors" to one's house. The correct translation seems to be "the needy"—those who visit a house to request food or other necessities.

10. *Samyutta Nikaya I*: Kosala Samyutta: Pathama Aputtaka Sutta
11. *Anguttara Nikaya V*: Mundaraja Vagga: Sappurisa Sutta
12. *Digha Nikaya 3*: 31: Sigalovada Sutta
13. Ibid.

14. *Sutta Nipata*: Uraga Vagga
15. *Samyutta Nikaya I*: Kosala Samyutta: Appaka Sutta
16. Ibid.
17. *Samyutta Nikaya I*: Kosala Samyutta: Donapaka Sutta

Chapter Three

Epigraph taken from: *Anguttara Nikaya II*: Sotapatti Samyutta: Upannasa Sutta; *Anguttara Nikaya VIII*: Gotami Vagga: Vyagghapajja Sutta
Note: This epigraph combines the two sources given above. The first sentence of the epigraph is from Upannasa Sutta. Referring to his own enlightenment, Buddha made this statement in order to emphasize the motivation for achievement. The original Pali term *asantutthita kusalesu dhammesu* has been translated as "not to be content with what I have achieved." The phrase *kusalesu dhammesu* defies any direct translation. In context, this phrase means Buddha's achievements in his inner development, excluding the final achievement of enlightenment.

1. *Anguttara Nikaya III*: Maha Vagga: Titthayatana Sutta
2. Ibid.
3. Ibid.
4. *Anguttara Nikaya II*: Vassupanayika Vagga: Uposatha Sutta
5. *Anguttara Nikaya VIII*: Gotami Vagga: Vyagghapajja Sutta
6. *Digha Nikaya III*: 31: Sigalovada Sutta
7. *Anguttara Nikaya III*: Rathakara Vagga: Dutiya Papanika Sutta
8. *Sutta Nipata*: Culla Vagga: Mangala Sutta
9. *Sumangala Vilasini*: Brahmajala Sutta Vannana
10. *Sutta Nipata*: Uraga Vagga: Parabhava Sutta:
11. *Digha Nikaya III*: 31: Sigalovada Sutta
12. *Anguttara Nikaya VIII*: Uposatha Vagga: Anuruddha Manapakayika Sutta
13. *Samyutta Nikaya I*: Kosala Samyutta: Appamada Sutta
14. *Digha Nikaya III*: 31: Sigalovada Sutta
15. Ibid.
16. *Samyutta Nikaya I*: Kosala Samyutta: Kalyanamitta Sutta
17. Ibid.
18. *Dhammapada*: Verse 155
19. *Digha Nikaya III*: 31: Sigalovada Sutta

Chapter Four

Epigraph taken from: *Anguttara Nikaya IV: Pattakamma Vagga: Pattakamma Sutta*
Note: The Pali phrase *dullabho* (*du*="difficult"+*labho*="to obtain") has been translated as "achievable through effort." Taken with the positive adjectives "pleasant," "agreeable," and "charming," the adjective *dullabho* should convey a positive

connotation.

1. *Anguttara Nikaya IV*: Abhinna Vagga: Kula Sutta
2. *Anguttara Nikaya IV*: Pattakamma Vagga: Pattakamma Sutta
3. Ibid.
4. *Anguttara Nikaya IV*: Pattakamma Vagga: Pattakamma Sutta
5. Ibid.
6. Ibid.
7. *Anguttara Nikaya VIII*: Gotami Vagga: Vyagghapajja Sutta
8. *Digha Nikaya III*: 31: Sigalovada Sutta
9. *Samyutta Nikaya I*: Kosala Samyutta: Sattajatila Sutta
10. *Digha Nikaya III*: 31: Sigalovada Sutta
11. Ibid.
12. Ibid.
13. Ibid.
14. Ibid.
15. *Anguttara Nikaya VIII*: Gotami Vagga: Vyagghapajja Sutta
16. *Anguttara Nikaya IV*: Pattakamma Vagga: Anana Sutta
17. *Anguttara Nikaya VIII*: Gotami Vagga: Vyagghapajja Sutta
18. *Anguttara Nikaya IV*: Pattakamma Vagga: Pattakamma Sutta
19. Ibid.
20. Ibid.
21. *Sutta Nipata*: Culla Vagga: Mangala Sutta
22. *Dhammapada*: Verse 47
23. *Anguttara Nikaya III*: Bala Vagga: Bhaya Sutta
24. *Digha Nikaya III*: 31: Sigalovada Sutta
25. Ibid.
26. *Samyutta Nikaya 1*: Kosala Samyutta: Kalyanamitta Sutta
27. *Anguttara Nikaya VIII*: Gotami Vagga: Ujjaya Sutta
28. *Sutta Nipata*: Uraga Vagga: Parabhava Sutta
29. *Digha Nikaya III*: 31: Sigalovada Sutta
30. Ibid.
31. *Anguttara Nikaya VIII*: Gotami Vagga: Vyagghapajja Sutta
32. *Digha Nikaya III*: 31: Sigalovada Sutta
33. Ibid.
34. Ibid.

Chapter Five

Epigraph taken from: *Samyutta Nikaya I*: Kosala Samyutta: Sattajatila Sutta

1. *Sutta Nipata*: Uraga Vagga: Khaggavisana Sutta
2. *Samyutta Nikaya I*: Brahmana Samyutta: Sundarika Sutta
3. *Anguttara Nikaya 1*: Bala Vagga
4. *Sutta Nipata*: Uraga Vagga: Vasala Sutta

5. *Anguttara Nikaya VIII*: Gotami Vagga: Gotami Sutta
6. *Samyutta Nikaya 1*: Kosala Samyutta: Sattajatila Sutta
7. Ibid.
8. Ibid.
9. *Anguttara Nikaya III*: Bala Vagga: Bhaya Sutta
10. *Anguttara Nikaya IV*: Punnabhisanda Vagga: Pathama Samajiva Sutta

Chapter Six

Epigraph taken from: *Anguttara Nikaya IV*: Punnabhisanda Vagga: Pathama Samvasa Sutta
1. *Anguttara Nikaya IV*: Punnabhisanda Vagga: Pathama Samvasa Sutta
2. *Digha Nikaya III*: 31: Sigalovada Sutta
3. Ibid.
4. *Samyutta Nikaya V*: Sotapatti Samyutta: Veludvareyya Sutta
5. *Anguttara Nikaya 1*: Ekaka Vagga
6. *Anguttara Nikaya VII*: Avyakata Vagga: Sattabhariya Sutta
7. *Digha Nikaya III*: 31: Sigalovada Sutta
8. Ibid.
9. *Anguttara Nikaya VIII*: Gotami Vagga: Gotami Sutta
10. *Anguttara Nikaya VIII*: Uposatha Vagga: Nakulamatumanapakayika Sutta
11. *Digha Nikaya III*: 31: Sigalovada Sutta
12. *Anguttara Nikaya VII*: Avyakata Vagga: Sattabhariya Sutta
13. Ibid.

Chapter Seven

Epigraph taken from: *Anguttara Nikaya III*: Devaduta Vagga: Sabrahmaka Sutta
1. *Anguttara Nikaya VIII*: Gotami Vagga: Vyagghapajja Sutta
2. *Samyutta Nikaya I*: Brahmana Samyutta: Mahasala Sutta
3. *Samyutta Nikaya I*: Kosala Samyutta: Pathama Aputtaka Sutta
4. *Sutta Nipata*: Culla Vagga
5. *Digha Nikaya III*: 31
6. *Dhammapada*: Verse 129
7. *Dhammapada*: Verse 133
8. *Dhammapada*: Verse 158
9. *Digha Nikaya III*: 31: Sigalovada Sutta
10. *Majjhima Nikaya II*: 58: Abhaya Rajakumara Sutta
11. *Majjhima Nikaya II*: 61: Ambalatthika Rahulovada Sutta
12. *Sutta Nipata*: Culla Vagga

Chapter Eight

Epigraph taken from: *Anguttara Nikaya V*: Aghata Vagga: Codana Sutta

1. *Anguttara Nikaya V*: Sona Vagga: Subhasitavaca Sutta; *Anguttara Nikaya V*: Aghata Vagga: Codana Sutta
2. *Majjhima Nikaya I*: 27: Culahatthipadopama Sutta
3. *Anguttara Nikaya V*: Raja Vagga: Pathama Cakkanuvattana Sutta
4. *Dhammapadatthakatha*: Sahassa Vagga: Kisagotamiya Vatthu
5. *Dhammapadatthakatha*: Sukha Vaggga: Annatarassa Upasakassa Vatthu
6. *Dhammapadatthakatha*: Citta Vagga: Putigattatissatthera Vatthu
7. *Anguttara Nikaya V*: Aghata Vagga: Codana Sutta
8. *Majjhima Nikaya II*: 58: Abhayarajakumara Sutta
9. Verse 232
10. *Sutta Nipata*: Cula Vagga: Hiri Sutta
11. *Anguttara Nikaya V*: Aghata Vagga: Codana Sutta
12. Ibid.
13. *Digha Nikaya I*: 8: Mahasihanada Sutta
14. *Anguttara Nikaya IV*: Indriya Vagga: Roga Sutta
15. *Anguttara Nikaya III*: Bala Vagga: Accaya Sutta
16. *Anguttara Nikaya III*: Puggala Vagga: Vajiropama Sutta
17. *Majjhima Nikaya II*: 86: Angulimala Sutta
18. *Anguttara Nikaya 1*: Ekaka Vagga: 1
19. *Anguttara Nikaya 1*: Ekaka Vagga: 2
20. *Anguttara Nikaya III*: Bala Vagga: Accaya Sutta
21. *Dhammapada*: Verse 329
22. *Majjhima Nikaya II*: 56: Upali Sutta
23. *Anguttara Nikaya VIII*: Gahapati Vagga: Hatthigamaka Ugga Sutta
24. *Anguttara Nikaya IV*: Kesi Vagga: Kesi Sutta
25. *Dhammapada*: Verse 3

Chapter Nine

Epigraph taken from: *Digha Nikaya I*: 4: Sonadanda Sutta; *Majjhima Nikaya II*: 96: Esukari Sutta

1. *Majjhima Nikaya II*: 96: Esukari Sutta
2. *Udana*: Sona Vagga: Uposatha Sutta
3. *Anguttara Nikaya VIII*: Gotami Samyutta: Gotami Sutta

Note: At the beginning of this conversation, Buddha's reluctance to permit the ordination of women is mostly due to social factors. An ordained disciple of Buddha had to practice meditation in solitude, often in a forest or in an empty house. In that society, such places were extremely dangerous for women. Apparently, Buddha did not want to cause problems for women by offering them ordination. However, after listening to Ananda's rational argument, Buddha agreed to offer ordination to women.

4. *Samyutta Nikaya V*: Bhikkhuni Samyutta: Soma Sutta
5. *Sutta Nipata*: Uraga Vagga: Vasala Sutta
6. *Majjhima Nikaya II*: 96: Esukari Sutta
7. *Anguttara Nikaya X*: Maha Vagga: Dutiya Mahapanna Sutta
8. *Majjhima Nikaya II*: 72: Aggivacchagotta Sutta
9. *Digha Nikaya*: *III*: 27: Agganna Sutta
10. Ibid.
11. *Majjhima Nikaya II*: 72: Aggivacchagotta Sutta
12. *Sutta Nipata*: Atthaka Vagga: Pasura Sutta
13. *Majjhima Nikaya II*: 58: Abhayarajakumara Sutta
14. *Majjhima Nikaya II*: 79: Culasakuludayi Sutta
15. *Digha Nikaya I*: 8: Mahasihanada Sutta

Chapter Ten

Epigraph taken from: *Anguttara Nikaya 1*: Ekadhamma Pali: Dutiya Vagga: 3-4
1. *Majjhima Nikaya II*: 95: Canki Sutta
2. Ibid.
3. *Majjhima Nikaya II*: 76: Sandaka Sutta
4. *Digha Nikaya I*: 13: Tevijja Sutta
5. *Digha Nikaya III*: 31: Sigalovada Sutta
6. *Digha Nikaya III*: 27: Agganna Sutta
7. Ibid.
8. *Majjhima Nikaya II*: 84: Madhura Sutta
9. *Digha Nikaya III: 27*: Agganna Sutta
10. *Digha Nikaya I*: 2: Samannaphala Sutta
11. *Samyutta Nikaya I* : Kosala Samyutta: Sattajatila Sutta
12. *Digha Nikaya I*: 4: Sonadanda Sutta
13. *Digha Nikaya I*: 11: Kevaddha Sutta
14. *Majjhima Nikaya II*: 76: Sandaka Sutta
15. *Digha Nikaya III*: 27
16. Ibid.
17. *Digha Nikaya 1*: 3: Ambattha Sutta
18. Ibid.
19. *Majjhima Nikaya II*: 92: Sela Sutta
20. Ibid.
21. *Majjhima Nikaya I*: 35: Culasaccaka Sutta
22. *Majjhima Nikaya II*: 56: Upali Sutta
23. *Majjhima Nikaya II*: 95: Canki Sutta
24. Ibid.
25. Ibid.
26. Ibid.

Chapter Eleven

Epigraph taken from: *Anguttara Nikaya III*: Maha Vagga: Kalama Sutta
1. *Digha Nikaya I*: 13: Tevijja Sutta
2. *Anguttara Nikaya III*: Maha Vagga: Kalama Sutta
3. *Digha Nikaya I*: 13: Tevijja Sutta
4. *Majjhima Nikaya II*: 98: Vasettha Sutta
5. *Anguttara Nikaya I*: Pamada Vagga: 5
6. *Dhammapada*: Verse 216
7. *Anguttara Nikaya III*: Ananda Vagga: Ananda Sutta
8. *Anguttara Nikaya III*: Maha Vagga: Akusalamula Sutta
9. *Anguttara Nikaya III*: Ananda Vagga: Ananda Sutta
10. *Dhammapada*: Verse 5
11. *Dhammapadatthakatha*: 1. 4: Kaliyakkhiniya Uppatti Vatthu
12. *Dhammapadatthakatha*: 15. 1: Kalahavupasamana Vatthu
13. *Anguttara Nikaya VII*: Abyakata Vagga: Kodhana Sutta
14. *Angutara Nikaya III*: Maha Vagga: Akusalamula Sutta
15. *Anguttara Nikaya III*: Ananda Vagga: Ananda Sutta
16. *Majjhima Nikaya II*: 82: Ratthapala Sutta
17. *Anguttara Nikaya III*: Ananda Vagga: Ananda Sutta
18. *Anguttara Nikaya III*: Maha Vagga: Akusalamula Sutta
19. *Anguttara Nikaya III*: Ananda Vagga: Ananda Sutta
20. *Majjhima Nikaya II*: 61: Ambalatthikarahulovada Sutta
21. *Anguttara Nikaya III*: Maha Vagga: Kalama Sutta

Chapter Twelve

Epigraph taken from: *Sutta Nipata*: Culla Vagga: Mangala Sutta
1. *Samyutta Nikaya V*: Sotapatti Samyutta: Veludvareyya Sutta
2. *Dhammapada*: Verse 182
3. *Vimanavatthu Atthakatha*: Rajjumala Vimana
4. *Anguttara Nikaya VII*: Avyakata Vagga: Kodhana Sutta
5. *Majjhima Nikaya III*: 144: Channovada Sutta; *Samyutta Nikaya III*: Khandha Samyutta: Vakkali Sutta
6. *Dhammapada*: Verse 131
7. *Digha Nikaya 1*: 5
8. *Anguttara Nikaya V*: Upasaka Vagga: Gihi Sutta
9. *Samyutta Nikaya V*: Sotapatti Samyutta: Veludvareyya Sutta
10. *Anguttara Nikaya I*: Cittapariyadana Vagga
11. *Anguttara Nikaya VIII*: Uposatha Vagga: Dutiyavisakha Sutta
12. *Samyutta Nikaya V*: Sotapatti Samyutta: Veludvareyya Sutta
13. *Majjima Nikaya I*: 41: Saleyyaka Sutta
14. *Digha Nikaya II*: 16: Mahaparinibbana Sutta

15. *Samyutta Nikaya IV*: Gamini Samyutta: Pataliya Sutta
Note: The Pali sentence *Ayam puriso . . . kulitthisu kulakumarisu carittam apajji* (This man got himself into sexual activity with protected women and girls) suggests forced sex.
16. *Anguttara Nikaya V*: Nivarana Vagga: Mataputta Sutta
17. *Digha Nikaya III*: 26: Cakkavattisihanada Sutta
18. *Anguttara Nikaya V*: Sona Vagga: Sona Sutta
19. *Anguttara Nikaya V*: Upasaka Vagga: Gihi Sutta
20. *Samyutta Nikaya V*: Sotapatti Samyutta: Veludvareyya Sutta
21. *Digha Nikaya I*: 8
22. *Anguttara Nikaya V*: Aghata Vagga: Codana Sutta
23. *Digha Nikaya III*: 31: Sigalovada Sutta
24. Ibid.
25. *Sutta Nipata*: Culla Vagga: Mangala Sutta
26. *Anguttara Nikaya IV*: Kesi Vagga: Kesi Sutta
27. *Digha Nikaya III*: 31: Sigalovada Sutta
28. *Majjhima Nikaya III*: 101: Devadaha Sutta
29. *Majjhima Nikaya III*: 112: Chabbisodana Sutta
30. *Majjhima Nikaya III*: 101: Devadaha Sutta
31. *Samyutta Nikaya V*: Sotapatti Samyutta: Veludvareyya Sutta
32. *Majjhima Nikaya III*: 101: Devadaha Sutta
33. Ibid.

Chapter Thirteen

Epigraph taken from: *Anguttara Nikaya III*: Bala Vagga: Lakkhana Sutta
1. *Digha Nikaya 1*: 4: Sonadanda Sutta
2. *Sutta Nipata*: Uraga Vagga: Vasala Sutta
3. *Anguttara Nikaya VI*: Maha Vagga: Nibbedhika Sutta
4. *Majjhima Nikaya II*: 61: Ambalatthikarahulovada Sutta
5. *Dhammapada*: Verse 252
6. *Anguttara Nikaya III*: Bala Vagga: Accaya Sutta
7. *Anguttara Nikaya III*: Puggala Vagga: Jigucchitabba Sutta
8. *Majjhima Nikaya 1*: 15: Anumana Sutta
9. Ibid.
10. *Majjhima Nikaya 1*: 10: Satipatthana Sutta
11. *Majjhima NIkaya 1*: 15: Anumana Sutta
12. *Majjhima Nikaya II*: 58: Abhayarajakumara Sutta
13. *Majjhima Nikaya II*: 61: Ambalatthikarahulovada Sutta
14. *Anguttara Nikaya VI*: Sacitta Vagga: Sariputta Sutta
15. *Majjhima Nikaya 1*: 15: Anumana Sutta
16. *Anguttara Nikaya III*: Sambodhi Vagga: Arakkhita Sutta
17. *Anguttara Nikaya III*: Bala Vagga: Cinta Sutta

18. *Dhammapada*: Verses 3-4

Chapter Fourteen

Epigraph taken from: *Dhammapada:* Verses 199 & 204

1. *Anguttara Nikaya I*: Pamada Vagga: 9
2. *Anguttara Nikaya III*: Devaduta Vagga, Hatthaka Sutta
Note: The Pali sentence is *yeca pana loke sukham senti so tesu aham accayo.*
Literally, *sukham senti* is "sleep happily," but its actual meaning is "live happily."
3. *Vinaya Pitaka*: Maha Vagga: 1. 11
4. Internet Edition of CNN news (Health), May 22, 2003
5. Internet Edition of BBC news, May 21, 2003
6. Ibid.
7. *Dhammapada*: Verse 165
8. *Dhammapada*: Verse 276
9. *Anguttara Nikaya III*: Maha Vagga: Titthayatana Sutta
10. *Proceedings of the National Academy of Sciences*, November 16, 2004
11. *Discoverychannel.com*: "Study: Meditation Changes Monks' Outlook." Anna Salleh, June 7, 2005
12. *Majjhima Nikaya II*: 79: Culasakuludayi Sutta
13. *Majjhima Nikaya III*: 86: Angulimala Sutta
14. *Samyutta Nikaya 1*: Devata Samyutta: Aranna Sutta
15. *Majjhima Nikaya III*: 132: Anandabhaddekaratta Sutta
16. *Dhammapada*: Verse 157
17. *Majjhima Nikaya I*: 18: Madhupindika Sutta
18. Ibid.
19. *Dhammapada*: Verse 216
20. *Dhammapada*: Verse 197
21. *Anguttara Nikaya 1*: Pabhassara Vagga: Pabhassara Sutta
22. *Majjhima Nikaya III*: 118: Anapanasati Sutta
23. Ibid.
24. *Digha Nikaya III*: 29: Pasadika Sutta
25. *Dhammapada*: Verse 198
26. *Dhammapada*: Verse 183
27. *Anguttara Nikaya IV*: Pattakamma Vagga: Anana Sutta
28. *Dhammapada*: Verse 69
29. *Samyutta Nikaya I*: Kosala Samyutta: Donapaka Sutta
30. *Dhammapada*: Verse 277
31. Ibid.

Index

Reader's notes